ULTIMATE GUIDE TO

Edited by John R. Little and Curtis F. Wong

New York Chicago San Francisco Lisbon London Madrid Mexico City
Milan New Delhi San Juan Seoul Singapore Sydney Toronto

Library of Congress Cataloging-in-Publication Data

Ultimate guide to paintball / edited by John R. Little and Curtis F. Wong.
      p.   cm.
    ISBN 0-8092-2549-2
    1. Paintball (Game)   I. Little, John R., 1960–.   II. Wong, Curtis.
  GV1202.S87 U48   2001
  796.2—dc21   00-59010
                                          CIP

5 6 7 8 9 10 11 12 13 14 15 16 17 18 19 20 21 22 23 24 25 26 27 28 VLP/VLP 0 9 8 7

ISBN-13: 978-0-8092-2549-1
ISBN-10:   0-8092-2549-2

Cover design by Marc Paez
Cover and interior photos are by Skirmish USA and Jessica J. Sparks and courtesy of CFW Enterprises, Inc.
Interior design by ABZORB Design, Inc.

McGraw-Hill books are available at special quantity discounts to use as premiums and sales promotions, or for use in corporate training programs. For more information, please write to the Director of Special Sales, Professional Publishing, McGraw-Hill, Two Penn Plaza, New York, NY 10121-2298. Or contact your local bookstore.

Disclaimer

This book is printed on acid-free paper.

Contents

Preface

Paintball! It's the newest action sport sweeping the world. Special air-powered markers and liquid-filled gelatin capsules bring new meaning to the game of Capture the Flag. Players numbering in the millions enjoy the fun and adrenaline thrills of paintball, week after week, throughout the United States and in more than 60 countries. Tournament competitions and festivals draw the best of teams and individuals to compete for championship titles.

Not surprisingly, such a spike in growth is paralleled only by an identical spike in the need for valid information. To this end, *Action Pursuit Games* magazine, founded in 1987, remains the "king of the hill," continuing to bring the latest developments in the world of paintball to its readers every month. I would be remiss if I did not single out the Herculean efforts of the senior advisor and former editor-in-chief of *Action Pursuit Games*, Jessica J. Sparks. Apart from her own articles (many of them reproduced in this volume), which reveal both innovation and an encyclopedic knowledge of the game, under her stewardship *Action Pursuit Games* became the leader of all paintball magazines.

Additional commendations are extended to all the writers and photographers who contributed to this book. They have an incalculable collective knowledge of paintball tactics and principles. This book represents the distilled knowledge of hundreds of man-years of study into every aspect and nuance of action pursuit games. Between the covers of this book are wisdom and experience that would cost a small fortune to obtain from one-on-one training with these writers. It is the thought, effort, and writing of these individuals that makes this book and *Action Pursuit Games* magazine great.

Ultimate Guide to Paintball brings you a special selection of articles from *Action Pursuit Games* covering subjects from how paintball began to winning tactics. It offers the strong knowledge base that every player needs.

Enjoy this inside look at paintball, a view through the eyes of those who know it best.

John R. Little

Who Plays Paintball?

The most recent Superstudy of Sports Participation by the Sporting Goods Manufacturers Association (SGMA) found that an estimated 5,923,000 Americans played paintball at least once in 1998. Of the participants, 74.4 percent were male and 25.6 percent were female, with an average player age of 19.

Paintball: The Living Video Game

Jessica J. Sparks

Paintball is a ticket to an ever-changing, always challenging, living video game. Nothing will substitute for the experience.

Paintball is an E-ride ticket to a special fantasy world. Try paintball, and odds are you'll play again and again. There are no substitutes. Players will tell you that "the worst day of paintball is better than the best day of anything else." People get hooked on the game, bitten by the paintball bug and high on its natural adrenaline.

Why?

Weekdays belong to work, school, traffic, dishes, shopping—and mundane demands fill all those hours. When we watch TV, we can only sit and applaud its daring action heroes who solve mysteries in a blaze of gunfire and its sport heroes who make game-winning plays. Along comes paintball, however, and we become *participants*. No longer couch potatoes, we're players in the game. Paintball quickly replaces vicarious thrills brought by an inanimate electronic box.

Paintball is incredibly challenging. It's a game where you become a sport hero. You become part of a living movie with a script that changes every minute—and what you do writes the script as you act. The challenge remains—always. About the time you start thinking how great you are, along comes some rookie who outfoxes you and hands you a dose of humility.

The game provides a total escape from whatever's bothering you. Can you worry about your bills when you're dodging flying paintballs? Try it.

A good friend of mine once said that paintball is "safe danger." He's right. Paintball is a game played with a 'gun that you use to "shoot" other people, and you get "shot" and live to tell about it over and over again. Like animated video-game figures, you lead a never-ending life. You "die"— but you don't. Each new game puts you back at

"Go" for a clean start in a new game. That's what happens when you shoot paintballs.

"Bonding" is a clinical name for teamwork and friendship. Whatever you choose to call this, you live it when you play paintball. You and your teammates work together toward a goal. To win the game each of you must find a balance between your individual initiative and the need to depend on each other.

This is an invitation to try paintball if you haven't already. All the words ever written about paintball will not substitute for the experience.

Paintball is safe danger.

Getting into Paintball

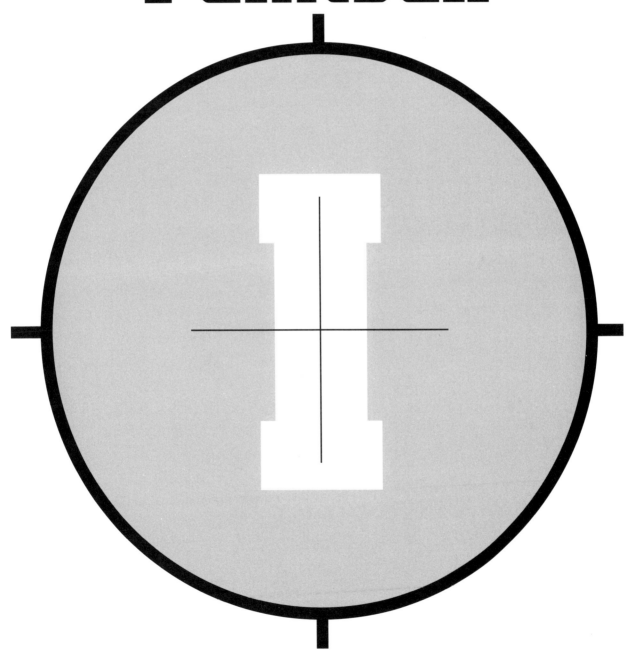

What Is Paintball?

Jessica J. Sparks

Paintball! It's recognized as one of the world's most exciting outdoor participation sports. Paintball is played in more than 60 countries by millions of people of different ages and lifestyles. Whether high school students or homemakers, professionals or retirees, paintball players share a love for adventure and a strong competitive spirit.

Paintball is a combination of the childhood games Tag and Hide and Seek, but it is much more challenging and sophisticated. Paintball is a sport played by people from all professions and lifestyles; women and men compete equally, and age is not dominated by youth. Physical size and strength are not as important as intelligence and determination. The ability to think quickly and decisively, as in a game of chess, is what will make you a star.

Paintball is also a character-building sport. Players learn the importance of teamwork and gain self-confidence while developing leadership abilities.

Paintball is an exciting sport, and above all paintball is fun. It's a chance to shake off your day-to-day responsibilities and rekindle your spirit of adventure. Once the adrenaline starts pumping, you can't help but love the thrill of the game!

How the Game Is Played

Although there are many different game formats, typically a group of players divides into two teams to play Capture the Flag. The object of the game is to capture the other team's flag and carry it back to your home base. While you are trying

Paintball is Tag and Hide and Seek all in one.

For safety, paintball players must always wear approved-for-paintball goggles and head-protection systems to protect the eyes and face during a game and while in other areas (such as the target range or chronograph area) where shooting is permitted.

Games have time limits, depending on the number of players and the size of the field. For smaller games of up to 25 on a side, the games usually have a time limit of 15 or 20 minutes. For games with more players, time limits may be 30 to 45 minutes per game. With teams of one to five players, games usually are from 3 to 10 minutes.

Referees on the field start and stop games, enforce the rules of fair play, and control the sport's safety. Paintball play sites have a referee staff and may run several games at the same time on different parts of the site. Each playing field has a marked boundary. A player who goes out-of-bounds is eliminated from that game.

to capture a flag, you also try to eliminate opposing players by tagging them with a paintball expelled from a special airgun called a *paintgun* or *marker*.

In the two-flag game, each of two teams starts from its own home base. The object of the game is to capture the other team's flag and hang it at your team's home base. In the one-flag game, a single flag is placed at an equal distance from each of two teams. The flag usually is in the center of the field. The object of the center flag game is to capture the flag and advance, carrying the flag to the opposing team's home base.

Paintball is usually played outdoors. Indoor play sites are becoming more common, usually in more urban areas. *Arenaball* (also called *speedball*) is paintball played in an arena (indoors or outdoors) where spectators can enjoy the excitement.

The number of players on each team can vary from four or five per team to more than five hundred on a side, the quantity limited only by the size of the playing field.

Both men and women compete equally in paintball.

Between games, players take a break to check their equipment, reload their paintballs, and have a snack or soda while they share stories about the thrills of victory and the (usually) funny agonies of defeat.

Win or lose, everyone has a good time, and there's always the next game waiting for you!

Paintballs

A paintball is a round capsule with colored liquid inside it. A paintball's thin outer shell is usually made of gelatin. Paintballs are similar to large, round vitamin capsules or bath-oil beads. The most common size of paintball is .68 inch in diameter. The fill inside a paintball is nontoxic, noncaustic, water soluble, and biodegradable. It

In the woods!

rinses out of clothing and washes off skin with mild soap and water.

Paintballs come in a rainbow of colors, such as blue, pink, white, orange, red, yellow, green, and other bright hues. The outer shell of a paintball may be a color swirl or two-toned. The inner fill of a paintball may be a different color than the outer shell.

When a paintball tags a player, the thin outer layer of the paintball splits open, and the liquid fill inside leaves a bright paint mark. A player who is marked is eliminated from the game. Usually the *mark* must be the size of a U.S. quarter to be considered big enough to eliminate the player. Smaller amounts of fill that mark a player are called *splatter* and usually do not eliminate the player.

Flags and Armbands

A flag as used in paintball is generally a rectangular piece of cloth about 24 by 12 inches in size. Players wear colored armbands to distinguish one team from another. In tournament games where each team has a flag to protect, usually a team's armband color will match the color of the flag its members are protecting. In recreational games the two flags should be of contrasting colors, or one should be patterned or striped, so that the flags do not look alike.

Paintguns (Markers)

Paintball markers (paintguns) come in a variety of shapes and styles, ranging from simple to sophisticated. *Stockguns* are powered by small 12-gram CO_2 powerlets that have to be changed after 15 to 25 shots. Nearly all stockguns are pumpguns. With a *pumpgun*, each time a player wants to shoot a paintball, the player must first cock the paintgun

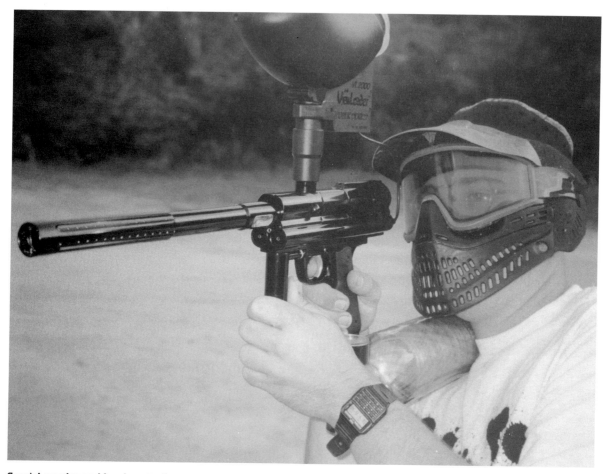

Special goggles and head-protection systems are mandatory.

by using a pump and then squeeze the trigger. The pumpgun must be recocked before the player can shoot again. Pumpguns may be powered by 12-gram (or larger) refillable CO_2 or compressed-air cylinders that supply hundreds of shots per fill.

Semiautomatic paintball markers are generally powered by refillable cylinders. With a semiauto, the player must first cock the paintgun in order to shoot a paintball. Then the mechanics of the paintgun will recock the paintgun, so that the next time the player squeezes the trigger, another paintball is shot. (With a fully automatic system,

in contrast, the mechanism is cocked once; then, if the trigger is squeezed and held down without release, the mechanism continues to shoot until the trigger is released.)

Safety

Paintball's superb safety record compared with other sports is mostly due to addressing safety concerns at the very beginnings of the game. Goggles and head-protection systems—designed for paintball and meeting specified standards—are always a requirement on any field, as are the use of barrel plugs and chronographs.

Barrel plugs are standard fare at all commercial fields. Once players leave the field of play, they are required to insert a barrel plug into the end of their barrel as a safety device to prevent injury if the marker is accidentally discharged in the neutral area. In tournament play, this rule is so strongly enforced as to cost the offending player's team penalty points if not observed.

Chronographs are another safety requirement. These devices that measure the velocity of a projectile have long been used for measuring the velocities of firearms' bullets, as well as the speed of arrows and other projectiles. In paintball the maximum velocity allowed worldwide is 300 feet per second (fps). This standard velocity limit may be, and often is, lowered to 275 fps or less for indoor or other close-range play. In tournament play, penalty points for exceeding the established speed limit have on many occasions cost a team a trip to the finals—or worse.

Referees start and stop every game and ensure that the safety regulations are observed. They tend to choose brightly colored clothing and headgear to distinguish themselves from players.

The information in this chapter is based, in large part, on "What Is Paintball?" originally developed and copyrighted by the nonprofit International Paintball Players Association, revised and reprinted by permission.

2

Bounced! Splatter! Out!
The Paintball Basics

Leland Jackson

"**I**'m out!"

He put his hand up over his head and left the field.

Remember how to play the game Tag? Whoever is "it" chases the other players until he or she can touch one of them. The touched player becomes it and the game goes on.

A paintball game is distantly related to the game of Tag. In paintball, though, there are two teams and everyone tries to tag out everyone who is on the opposing team. You tag them by marking them with paintballs shot from a special airgun called a paintball gun (also called a *paintgun* or a *marker*).

A tagged player is out; he or she has to leave the game field. The more players you tag out, the easier it is for your team to achieve the game's main goal of capturing your opponents' flag. How do you know when you have tagged an opponent?

He or she gives an "elimination signal" and leaves the field. The signal says to the shooter, "Good shot!" In tournament paintball, all or part of your score comes from counting the number of opponents your team eliminates or tags out.

Those few rules are the basis for the game. Paintball keeps growing because it's a lot of fun to play. The game is fun because the rules are simple and easy to understand. Here's a more in-depth look at these rules.

Out!

The basic, universally accepted elimination signals are verbal, visual, or both. A *verbal signal* is saying "I'm hit!" or "I'm out!" or "Good shot, coming out!" or "Dead man!" These are words that make it very clear that the speaker has been tagged and is coming out of the game. A *visual signal* is raising one hand over your head, raising your paintgun over your head, or a combination of the two. Other accepted visual signals used less often are putting a barrel plug into the muzzle of your marker, putting a white sock over the end of the barrel, or putting on an orange vest. Still another visual signal is walking with other eliminated players. "If you walk with the dead, you catch their disease" is how Joe Ecklund at SC Village in southern California puts it.

At the safety briefing given before the games begin, you should hear the rules for how to call yourself out. Players are expected to stop shooting at someone who is giving an "I'm out!" signal.

When you play in a paintball tournament, you might find slightly different rules for calling yourself out. Some tournament rules allow only visual elimination signals (no verbal signals) because that adds to the challenge of the games; players have to pay close attention to who's in and who's out. Even under these rules, players can verbally call themselves out to keep from getting pounded or for other safety reasons.

Stop Shooting!

Once you have called yourself out (visually or verbally), your opponents are supposed to stop shooting at you. It is poor sportsmanship to keep shooting at a player who has called himself out. At some fields if you keep shooting a "dead" player, the referees may eliminate you from the game, too. Good sportsmanship says that when you see a paintball mark an opponent, you stop shooting at the player—even if he or she didn't call him- or herself out yet.

Raise your arm and paintgun high to signal "Out!"

So what do you do if the opponent doesn't stop shooting? Tell the player he is hit: "Hey, you're hit on the pouch!" or "Buddy, check your right shoulder; you're hit!" Stop shooting at him while he checks. If he won't stop shooting and check himself, call a referee to go check the player. The ref will tell him to leave the game.

Now, that's what happens in a perfect world. But in paintball, you're going to meet players who say things like "Hey, if he won't call it, I'm not going to quit shooting until he does." There's a real problem with carrying around this attitude—deliberately overshooting someone takes the fun out of his game. And overshooting is a bad habit to get into because there are fields that enforce a three-break rule (if a shooter breaks more than two paintballs on someone, the shooter leaves the game with him).

Plus, lots of times you may be absolutely positive that you hit someone, but she's not marked.

The light, the shadows, old paint marks, splatter, or your imagination and adrenaline can make you believe every paintball you shoot must have broken on someone. Call for a paintcheck. And, by the way, it's not a good idea to accuse someone of cheating by yelling at the top of your lungs, "Hey, quit wiping!" Get a paintcheck on the player instead of accusing him.

A word of warning on this for players thinking about playing in tournaments: You can find recreational-level tournaments, where things are pretty much played like walk-on games. Mainly what you will find, though, are hard-core (and harder) tourneys. In hard-core ball, players stay on the trigger longer. Often you have to call yourself out fast to avoid taking multiple hits.

Bounced!

When you're hit but the ball didn't mark you, a good sport lets his opponent know what happened. Call out "Bounced!" or "Didn't break!" or "Splatter!" It's good sportsmanship.

New players often goof when they take a bouncer. They call themselves out when they feel a hit. They fail to check themselves to see if the ball actually marked them. The gelatin skin of a paintball has to split open to let out the colored fill. It's the fill that leaves the mark. Check before you call yourself out.

Once you call yourself out, you must leave the game. The experienced players will enforce this rule on you. If you call "Hit!" and then you look and say "Oh, it didn't break!" you may very well hear a voice from the bushes say "You called it, buddy, you have to leave!" Leave the game. Next time, though, check first.

Paintcheck

If you think you tagged someone who is not calling himself out, call "Paintcheck!" This tells the referees that you want someone to be checked. You also have to tell the ref where he is ("Ref, check that player behind the rocks!"). It's poor sportsmanship to try to use a ref to locate a player, meaning you don't know where someone is, so you just shoot into a big area and ask the ref to "Check him!" Experienced referees will ask you where the opponent is, specifically, and if you can't tell them, they don't go hunting. Refs who know what you're trying to pull will look around and tell you "He's clean!" even when no one is there.

If you think that you are marked but can't tell for sure, call a paintcheck on yourself. Call "Paintcheck! Here, ref!" and wait for the ref to come over and check. You must stop shooting. You must stop all aggressive action. You may run to cover and wait for the ref. After you're checked, you can resume playing if you are clean.

Out Is Out

It's cheating to signal you are out of the game and then to play on. Once you call yourself out, you must leave the game.

Dead Man's Walk

Watch out for the play called a "dead man's walk." It is a legitimate but sneaky play in which a player acts as if he's out. His body language says, "Oh, man, rats, I'm out!" but, really, he is not marked. He might carry his paintgun by the barrel at his

The more players that are tagged out, the easier it is to get the flag.

side (without putting in his barrel plug). He might walk through the opponents' skirmish line until he gets behind them—then he can pull the flag or start shooting opponents from behind. The dead man's walk is a legal play unless a field's rules strictly prohibit it.

But the player is cheating if she gives an elimination signal (raises hand or marker, puts barrel plug in, verbally calls himself out, etc.) and then tries to pull off a dead man's walk. Remember, once you give an elimination signal, you must leave the game. Also, someone is cheating if he walks with eliminated players to pretend he is hit when he isn't. Remember, "If you walk with the dead, you catch their disease."

Why can't you use elimination signals as a deceptive game tactic? Safety, for one thing. When you see an elimination signal, you must stop shooting at that player. She's hit, or he wants to surrender, and there is no call to shoot again. He may need to get off the field for other reasons (goggle fogging, doesn't feel good, etc.); his signal tells you "Stop shooting!" so he can leave. Players need to know they can always leave a game by giving an elimination signal.

Another reason is that the player doing a dead man's walk usually ends up close to, or behind, his or her opponents. This means it's likely for those opponents to get shot close up or in the back—and getting hit like that tends to upset players and cause verbal confrontations. Paintball rules are designed to avoid creating hard feelings that lead to verbal confrontations.

How do you spot a dead man's walk? Look for someone who does not have his or her 'gun or hand up. Challenge this opponent: "Hey, are you out?" If he or she does not say "Yes!" pretty fast, or raise a hand or 'gun, generally you are free to shoot. (If he's obviously a new player, ask him again before you shoot—give him a break—new players don't remember all the rules.)

If the person you just shot yells at you ("Hey! I'm out!") because she really is out, tell her "Hey, you didn't have your hand up!" to remind her about the rules. Next time she will keep her 'gun or hand up. (Take it easy on new players who don't always remember all the rules.)

Leaving

A player may have a reason for wanting to leave a game other than because of being hit. Maybe his or her marker isn't working right. Or he's out of paint or air. Or her pager just went off. Maybe he found himself in a bad spot and decided it wasn't worth staying in when he's about to get smoked.

You don't always know *why* someone is giving an elimination signal. Always respect the signal and let that player out quickly and safely. That's good sportsmanship—and good safety.

3

Newbie, Repent!

James R. "Mad Dog" Morgan, Sr.

The sounds of organ music greet you. "Welcome! Welcome, dear first-time players and dear people who are just considering the sport of paintball. Allow me to introduce myself. I'm Brother Mad Dog. I'm one of the few people who devote energy and time to those who are among the newest of our brethren in paintball. Today, my message is for *you,* the newbie player. It's designed to help you become a recreational player and forever leave behind the label 'newbie.'"

First of all, let's clear up a misunderstanding. Being a newbie is not and has never been a sin, contrary to how some "veteran" paintball players joke in the staging area. It is no fault of a newbie if he or she lacks the proper knowledge of all paintball equipment, tactics, and strategies (it does not miraculously come into your head the first time you sign the insurance paperwork on your first day of paintball). Those guys who've been

playing for years have simply forgotten how they, too, were once as innocent and apprehensive as you are now. Even those players who show natural ability from the start must endure a few days of trial and error to learn the things necessary to become an accepted veteran "paintdog."

Although being a newbie is not a sin, there are several things first-time players do that fall into the innocently sinful category. These should be addressed. Newbies need to know the ways to repent their poor doings (and avoid them).

Let's begin the lessons.

Dress

Dress correctly for your day of paintball. Don't look like you've fallen off the turnip truck or out of the executive boardroom. I'm not telling you to go out and buy yourself some exotic and expensive camouflage, but there are some clothes that scream "dead meat" to a veteran.

What not to wear is a short-sleeved shirt (especially in certain colors such as red, yellow, white, or pink). You have to wear something with long sleeves to cover and protect your arms. What not to wear in long sleeves are the shirts that say you've been to Disney World, attended Old Ivy University, or support the local sport team. Choose a long-sleeved, one-color sweatshirt, preferably in black, brown, or dark green.

What not to wear in pants is an old, faded pair of jeans. That, more than anything else, screams "newbie alert" to the veterans. And don't wear shorts and knee socks (to avoid becoming the butt of a couple of jokes). Your best bet is to visit a local surplus store and get a used pair of camouflage pants in woodland. The store will tell you which pattern is "woodland."

What not to wear in shoes are street shoes, deck shoes, or cowboy boots. The most common injury to players is a sprained ankle, so wear some-

Dress like you have experience.

thing with ankle protection: hiking boots or high-top athletic footwear.

Why does it matter how you look? If you don't look like a newbie, you won't be treated like one. Let me mention one little paintball irony. I've seen the situations reversed. I've witnessed cases where top amateurs and pros have shown up at fields wearing just what I'm telling you not to wear. They really give a working over to those players who don't know who they're dealing with and expect to get an easy "kill." They think they're dealing with a joker who's a rank amateur—and they are really up against someone who plays for one of the best teams in the world.

How to Act

Once you have the right look, the next step is not to act like a first-time player. Remember, veterans can smell fear, so act confident and self-assured. Come to play with the proper mind-set.

Being a newbie is not, and never has been, a sin.

I always come to the field with a positive attitude, knowing I'm going to have a great time and do really great things on the field. I'm not cocky, but having the proper mind-set really does help. My playing has improved since I changed my attitude coming into the field.

Show No Fear We need to address something related to self-confidence: Don't let yourself be intimidated by veteran players. You know the scene—you've just sat down and are getting familiar with your rental equipment when some hotshot moseys by holding a paintgun with a custom paint job, packing a scope (maybe even a laser sight), and dressed from head to toe in some sort of exotic camouflage worn by an elite military unit. He proceeds to the target range and puts five or six rounds within a couple inches of each other on

Act confident and self-assured.

the farthest target, and then he complains that his sights are off. That's intimidation!

Players like that may be good, but as I always say, "It's not the wrapper; it's what's inside that counts." Sure, he may be able to shoot paint accurately at the target range, but those targets aren't shooting back. He may be dressed in the best camouflage you've ever seen . . . but wouldn't you like to see what your paintball looks like on it? If you tell yourself that he's not going to have much trouble eliminating you, then that's what's going to happen. In effect, you've made it easier for him to do it. If, on the other hand, you think "Okay, he's got better equipment and more experience, but he's going to have to earn my scalp," then you've successfully countered his intimidation.

When someone tries to intimidate you, spend less time looking at what he wants you to look at. Instead, look for where he's weakest. If you find a flaw and exploit it, then he'll be the one avoiding you, not vice versa. It's most enjoyable when you take out an ego or two a weekend.

Gear and Field

Now, it's time to think about getting familiar with equipment and the field. If you've never played this particular field, arrive early and ask if you can walk the field before the games start. You may be asked to wear goggles while you are on the field— do it. This way, you'll have an idea of where the cover is best and where it's nonexistent, without having to waste valuable game time finding it out (many times to your detriment).

Next, you need to familiarize yourself with the equipment. Take the paintgun to the target or chronograph range and spend more than just a dozen balls to find out how accurate the 'gun is.

Get used to your equipment so you can focus
on the game.

Practice until you're reasonably confident you can
hit what you aim at.

During this time, if you have a problem with
the paintgun or don't know how something on it
works, ask one of the field staff to help you. You
may need to take the 'gun back to the rental
shack. The idea is for you to become confident
using your paintgun. You'll be ready to deal with
the paintgun if a problem shows up when you're
in the middle of your first game. Instead of having not the wildest notion of what to do, you'll
have an idea of how to solve the problem.

If the field rents squeegees, then it's a good
idea to get one. Sometimes refs carry them, but
you're better off with your own. Broken balls in
the paintgun are a very common problem for newbies. Paint in the barrel takes your accuracy right
out the window and makes hitting your target a
matter of luck, not skill. If you suspect that a
paintball has broken in the barrel (hint: your paintballs do wild curves after they leave the barrel

when the barrel is wet), use the squeegee or have
the referee squeegee the barrel for you. All veteran players carry them. Having your own
squeegee will keep you on par with the vets in this
category.

Tactics

Now, let's get to tactics. You don't need to be a
graduate of the "Green Beret" or "Marine Sniper"
school to use a few basic tactics to good effect.

Simple tactics are the easiest to use, and, as a
general rule, must be countered by simple tactics
from the other side. First, if you're in a group,
don't bunch up. Too many times a group of newbies do a thing I've nicknamed "Sheep Awaiting
Slaughter." They stay together with only a few feet
separating each one of them. This makes it so easy
for the opposing players to flank them on three
sides and just pour in paint on them. It's not a
pretty sight.

Bunching up creates a bigger target.

Take real estate when the game starts.

Skirmish Line

If you want to stay together, that's fine, but you need to do it the right way. Form a skirmish line. In effect, you proceed down the field in a line across the field, leaving at least 10 to 12 feet between each player. This makes your group much harder to flank. Also, if you encounter anyone, the people to the left and right of you can help take out the opponent you encountered. Any single player in the path of a skirmish line usually finds himself in a crossfire. He's usually going to have a spectator ticket handed to him quickly.

When you're part of a skirmish line, keep communicating with your teammates to the right and left. Communication and teamwork are two components of paintball that, if practiced, make you a much better player.

Free Land

Next, when a game starts, go out running and take as much territory as you can while it's still free. Those of you who come out of the gate slow may have to face opposition that has already taken two-thirds of the field. In other words, try to play on the other team's half of the field. That limits its space and makes it much harder for the opponents to get to your flag.

By scouting the field before the game, you already have a pretty good idea of where the middle of the field is. That's where you're likely to meet (make contact with) the opponents right after the game starts.

Game Plan

Before the game starts, have the team agree on some simple plan. For example, you may want to put more of your players on the left side, the right side, or in the center to break through opponents' defenses. Briefly figure out who is going to take the key objectives (the good places where you want to be when the paint starts flying). Ask what favorite tactics have been used on this field (any veteran players on your side can tell you what the moves are).

Relax

Most important, relax and think. Too many newbies let their adrenaline do the talking. They shoot anything that moves (only to find out it's a teammate).

Paintball is a thinking person's sport as much as it is a "jock" sport. How else can you explain how players in wheelchairs, on crutches, or using prosthetic limbs play this sport so well? Paintball is one sport where nerds take out linebackers. The adrenaline and thrill of playing are part of why we play the game, but letting them get the better of us negatively affects our playing abilities. To state a simple fact, you will make fewer mistakes if you think more and shoot less.

Relax, think—and you'll send "spectator tickets" to the experienced players.

Commandments

And as I conclude this sermon, I leave you, my happy flock, with certain basic rules of play.

1. Thou shalt always wear approved eye and head protection whilst in any paintball shooting area.
2. Thou shalt use barrel plugs whilst not in shooting areas.
3. Thou shalt never shoot a paintgun at a velocity over the field's speed limit, which must never exceed 300 fps.
4. Thou shalt never brandish a paintgun in public.
5. Thou shalt never misuse thy paintgun.
6. Thou shalt keep thy ears open and mouth shut during the safety lecture.
7. Thou shalt never mix paintball with alcohol or controlled substances, before or during play.
8. Thou shalt control thy temper during play.

9. Thou shalt inspect and replace the lenses on thy paintball goggles as directed by the manufacturer's instructions.
10. Do unto all players, newbies included, as you would have them do unto you.

Onward

By making an effort to improve yourself, and taking good advice from Brother Mad Dog, your play will improve. Soon you will need to remember, when your friends razz the newbies, that you were only ever so recently one of them. Show newbies compassion. They are wearing the shoes you so recently wore.

Newbies no more

This Is Paintball

Nathan "Nobody" Greenman

Ahot and windy day. The leaves in the trees rustled angrily, while distant birds sang happily. I was trying to stay calm and keep a cool head. We had already lost Darren, Chris, Tom, and Pat the first time we went for the flag. We lost Pete and Eric the second time. All we'd accomplished was to eliminate more of them than they did of us. And there wasn't much time.

"Get your head down!"

Just as Randy got his head down, a burst of paintballs flew by. Lucky I saw him in time. He almost took us out.

"He's in a good spot. He could pick us off," I mumbled. I'll never forget what Randy said next: "Nathan, let me charge him! He'll get me, but I'll take him out!"

"Are you crazy?" I said.

Randy answered, "Let me use my speed to get up close before he sees me. I know I can take him out, and I know he'll get me, but there are four of us and only two of them. If I take this guy out, we win."

Do you have the instincts to survive?

23

We dress like futuristic warriors.

Briefly, I hesitated. "Maybe we could do this without having to lose a man." Then reason took over, and I knew this is what Randy's good at. This is what he does. I know it sounds horrible, but sometimes the end does justify the means. Sometimes the good of the group comes before the good of one individual.

"Go! Go! Go!" I shouted. I stood up and started shooting as fast as I could. Randy ran toward our prey. All he needed to do was get far enough to sneak a shot around the side of the bunker.

Teamwork and skill will get that flag.

I saw Randy's target stick his 'gun out from behind his bunker. Randy opened up. He has one of the fastest trigger fingers in the business. His intimidating burst of rounds made our soon-to-be victim hesitate. With that, Randy bought himself the time he needed. As he rounded the bunker, I heard their two 'guns chase each other. Randy and our target walked off the field. Our plan had worked.

That's right. They walked off the field. They walked off the field together because this is only a game. This is paintball.

We dress like futuristic warriors: head gear; high-tech, air-powered paintguns; and camouflage. Every detail, no matter how small, might buy you that split-second advantage—that edge that separates the predator from the prey.

We shoot round balls of paint at each other. The gelatin shell of a paintball splits open when the paintball hits its target. The colored fill marks a player, and he's "eliminated." Yes, it hurts a little bit when the paintball tags you—not a lot, sometimes not much at all. Once in a while it stings a bunch. But potential pain and the thrill of "safe danger" are the mothers of adrenaline. This is a game that calls upon your survival instincts. This is the closest that you will ever get to the real thrill of "hunt or be hunted." Yet, this game is not about hurting.

Paintball is one of the safest sports in the world. It is safer than bowling, fishing, and a host of other noncontact sports. Think about it. Paintball is one of the most intense, action-packed games you will ever see, yet it is also one of the safest. If you think it's satisfying to win a round of streetfighter on your video game, you should try paintball.

The only battle wound that Randy got was a little round bruise the size of a quarter. He experienced all the adrenaline of a life-sacrificing charge, and walked away with only a bruise. And the person who Randy had to take out? A young player, 14 years old, already a well-recognized player who holds his own against anyone. Many

We shoot round balls of paint at each other.

paintball players in their 60s are very skilled, too. This sport is open to everyone. In fact, the big players who may be great athletes make easier targets. It is not muscle that wins the day—it is brains!

Paintball is life-size, living chess. Hunt or be hunted. Predator or prey. Hunt to your heart's content, but not just in your head or on a game board. Use your body, use your head, and use an acre of land. Set your team's players into positions

Will you play an aggressive game?

and see if they can eliminate the opposition. See if they dare the risk of taking "key" positions. Some of your players can move fast. Some can "kill" from a distance. You learn to use all you have to conquer your opponents and take their flag. Will you start out in a defensive posture and let them come to you, or will you be part of an aggressive team and go right at them?

Your opposition is equally armed, each player with his or her individual strengths and weaknesses. The playing field is even, aside from individual abilities. Come on, join in the fun! Do you have the instincts to survive and the courage to conquer?

Camouflage might buy a split-second advantage.

Inside the Rules

Dan Reeves

The general rules of paintball are pretty much the same everywhere. What you're about to read are general rules. You may find a few variations where you play, though, so if your field does things a little differently, don't be surprised and don't assume that your field isn't doing things "right."

Let's start with the basics. You're going to play Capture the Flag, with two teams participating, each with its own color for armbands. Each team will start from a flag station. The field has marked boundaries. The game has a time limit. What else do you need to know about the playing rules? The rules of the game are usually discussed in the orientation meeting, so listen closely.

Armbands

What colors will each team wear? Usually they are worn on the left arm, and are not to be covered up with clothing. A common mistake new players make is to shoot whatever moves—before looking to see what armband the player has or asking, for example, "Are you blue?"

Can you lie about your color? Usually, yes. This used to be a big deal—on some fields if you said "I'm blue" when you had on a red armband, you were out of the game for lying about your color. You could say "I'm your color," "What's *your* color?" or anything that wasn't a direct lie—and that was all right. The "can't lie about your color" rule does exist, but since it is not very different from no rule at all about what you can say, it's the rare field where you find this rule in use.

"Friendly Fire"

That's what you call it when a teammate is shot by his own team. It usually happens for one of three reasons: (a) you get mixed up and think your

Tournaments are for fun and prizes.

waited silently, seeing yet another target approaching, suddenly there was a WHAP! WHAP! Two balls to the posterior. Friendly fire. She left the field, grumbling.

Elimination Mark

How much paint do you have to put on someone before he's out of the game? The rule used most often is a quarter-size splat. Less than that and you are not out, even if the ball hit you and broke (but didn't leave enough paint). A few fields, however, may use a dime-size or a nickel-size as the objective measure.

This rule works for two reasons: (a) it keeps players from being called out on splatter (little bits of paint on you that did not come from a hit), and (b) it is neutral and fair to all. A ref looks at paint on you and sees the size of the splat. Smaller than a quarter, it's splatter and you're not out. Everyone is in or out by the same measuring stick. Easy! Every field worldwide ought to use this rule. It's been used for international tournaments, and it works. It takes a tremendous amount of guesswork and a number of arbitrary calls out of the referee arena. A ref who wants to be technical can carry a quarter to check size against.

This topic gets confusing when people don't think it through. "Well, if the ref sees the ball hit you and it leaves any paint at all, you're out" is a variation you may encounter, but that really is unfair. If you are next to a ref and a ball hits you but leaves only a little paint, you're out because the ref saw the ball hit you—but the guy you hit with no ref to see the ball hit him can have the same amount of paint on him that you do and get to stay in. Not fair.

teammate is on the other team, (b) you don't look for an armband or ask, or (c) your teammate has become totally confused and is going the "wrong way" on the field. The question is whether it counts. If so, he's out. If not, he's not out. It is rare these days to find a game where friendly fire does not count.

A real key to telling who's on your team is which direction the player's gun is pointing. Not too long ago, a player on the frontline engaged in three firefights with the other team, taking out two opponents. She dropped to the ground, since the cover wasn't very good, and belly-crawled forward a few feet so she could see the left tape and cover a kill zone. Behind her, about 50 feet back and slightly to her left nearer the wire, three new players on her own team were behind a bush. They had stayed hunkered down while the more experienced players were in action. As she

Paintgun Hits

Do 'gun hits count? In other words, if the ball hits your 'gun, are you out? For tournaments, the answer is 99.9 percent "yes"—worldwide. For walk-on games, the answer can be whatever the field wants it to be. "They don't count" is an excellent rule for fun. If the field owner wants his or her customers on the field, playing lots of paintball and having a good time, then the better rule is "'Gun hits do not count." You get more time on the field this way—it's a win for players and a win for field owners.

Splatter

If the ball breaks on something besides you and splatters on you, are you out? Usually you're not. You may have to show the ref what the ball hit first (a rock, a tree, a wall) but most of the time a ref can tell. If gun hits do not count as discussed in the previous section, you will have to show the ref where the ball broke on your gun to prove that paint on you is from a gun hit.

The thing with splatter is that it can be heavy enough to look like a hit, and it can accumulate (splatter, splatter, splatter, and pretty soon you have enough paint on you to look like a hit; if that happens, you might get called out on splatter). Be prepared to show the ref what the ball hit and broke on before it splattered onto you. If you're getting splattered, call a ref over: "Ref, I'm taking a lot of splatter!" The ref can see that it's only splatter and should not call you out for that paint being on you. Accept the fact that now and again you may be called out on splatter, but it happens to everyone if you play long enough. It's part of

Surrender is an option.

the game. When you are a ref, remember what it feels like to get called out on splatter before you make that judgment call.

"Out" Calls

If you're hit, the ball broke, and clearly you are to leave the game, you should signal that you're leaving so you don't keep getting hit. There are visual and verbal elimination signals. A signal of either kind should be respected and accepted as a sign that the player is saying "Stop shooting, I'm hit, and I'm leaving the field. See you next game."

The visual signal that means "I'm out!" and works everywhere in the world is to raise your hand and arm over your head. You can raise your 'gun over your head (along with your hand and arm). The two other visual signals that are widely used are (a) taking off your armband, and (b) putting in your barrel plug. These last two signals are not so easy to see and so are better used after you put your hand up.

The verbal signal most used is "I'm out!" Other verbal signals are "Dead man!" or "Hit!"

Because the game can be noisy, or played on big fields, or played with people who are hearing-impaired, it is best to use a visual signal (unless you're in so tight somewhere that all you can do is yell to let people know to stop shooting at you). Of course, once you call yourself out using any one of these signals, you cannot go back into the game—not even if the ball bounced.

Every few years someone drags a bad idea out of the closet and tries to make players follow a "magic word" rule. It doesn't work. A manager might say, "You are out only if you say the magic word *out* or the magic word *hit*, and until you say the magic word, people can keep shooting at you." This is not a good type of rule: using it, if you get hit in the middle of a hot game and yell "Dead man!" the other players can keep right on shooting at you. Not fun. Not a good rule.

Surrendering is another way to call yourself out. When asked to surrender, simply raise your hand, say "I give up," or use one of the above ways to call yourself out. If you don't do this quickly, you are likely to be shot and probably from a fairly close range. The decision is yours; use common sense. Fields have different surrender rules such as "If you are within *x* feet of someone you must ask him to surrender," or "If you get within *x* feet of someone he has to surrender," but these vary a lot from field to field. The basic common courtesy is to ask for the surrender, but stay prepared to shoot if the person won't give in. Shoot him in a less sensitive area, like the pods.

Head Shots

Avoid head shots. That's a universal safety rule.

Head shots do "count" at the world's fields today. Long ago, some fields were played under a rule that "head shots don't count" and some people also said, "If you shoot someone in the head, you (the shooter) are out and the guy you hit is still in" (sometimes both of you were out). Imagine how that used to be: you could get hit in the goggles or hit in the head over and over and still "get" to stay in the game. You could aim for someone's body but have really lousy paint or the guy might move, and *whap!* You hit him in the head and you're out. It wasn't fair, and it led to disagreeable situations.

Paintchecks

"Call a paintcheck" means two things to a player. If you think you broke a ball on someone, you call

Avoid taking deliberate head shots.

Referees check players for paint marks.

to a referee "Paintcheck!" or "Paintcheck on that man behind the wall, ref, please!" If you think you've been hit but can't see the area where the ball hit you (such as on your back), you call to a referee "Paintcheck over here, ref!" and get yourself checked. That's how simple it is.

What not to do? Do not turn into a broken "checkit" who keeps sounding off, "Check him ref, checkit, checkit, check him, ref!" Save your paintchecks for the times when you really think you hit the guy. For ones you call on yourself, try to find out if you're hit by lightly touching the area where you felt the ball hit. If you find paint on your hand, it broke; you're out, so leave the field.

Informal paintchecks are different from those where a ref is involved. They are when you call out to the other guy and ask him to check himself: "Check your leg!" will work. If he won't check or if you don't think he saw the break, then get a ref involved.

Chronograph Speed Limits

The universal speed limit is 300 feet per second for industry-standard .68-caliber paintguns. The speed is measured by a chronograph (there are several brands of chronos). "Shooting hot" means the 'gun is sending paintballs out at a speed faster than the field's speed limit. A field can have a lower speed limit for all players, usually 280 to 290 fps. Games with new or young players may have all the guns at a slower speed. Tournaments generally run at 300 fps.

Indoors, speeds may be restricted to less than 250 fps, and even as low as 200 fps for really tight and up-close scenarios. The paintballs split open at low speeds (but they bounce a lot). At many indoor fields where lighting is dim (and for night games), people play by the rule "If the ball hits you, you are out whether it broke or not." That rule calls for honor among players, but except for the occasional cheater, players will call themselves out.

Wear full head protection: It's required!

Having a speed limit puts a limit on how hard balls will hit (in other words, limits the impact energy of the paintball). Ask a math or physics teacher if you don't know about this and want a technical explanation. Don't think that faster means better. Too fast, and some paint tends to burst inside the barrel, while other shots show a flight path that may curve or "wing."

A player who gets caught adjusting his velocity on the field can expect to be sent off the field immediately, and may be sent home for the day. Turning your 'gun up creates a safety hazard. Check your 'gun after you do anything that might change its velocity (new air fill, changing a part, changing a barrel, etc.).

Do I Have to Wear a Face Mask?

Yes, and you should. Don't you like your face? Why wouldn't you? And don't just wear a face mask; today's insurance rules mandate that players wear the goggle- and head-protection system that helps protect the temple, sides of the head, and neck as well as the front of your face (which includes your eyes, nose, lips, and mouth).

Chronographing

Speedball games can take place in the woods.

big cylinders)—so you can take any semiauto, pumpgun, or stockgun into the game. Fully automatic paintguns (yes, there are a couple) may be allowed (usually they are not), but it's better to call ahead and ask. Other games might allow pumpguns only (constant-air or 12-gram pumpguns) or 12-gram only.

Start-of-Game Signal

A game may be started with a whistle, a bullhorn, a call ("Game on!"), or a combination of these noisemakers. The signal needs to be heard simultaneously by both teams. Along with a sound signal, a visual signal may be used. For example, a ref in the center of the field—in sight of both teams—could hold a towel over his head; when he drops his arm and brings the towel down, the game starts. At some tournaments, only a visual signal is used. When hearing-impaired players are on the field, a visual signal must be used.

There may be a referee's warning ("Game starts in one minute") or a referee's countdown ("5-4-3-2-1, Game on!"). Or, especially at tournaments, the ref may say "One-minute warning"—and the game can start anytime from then on, at the whim of the ref who starts the game.

When you are playing on a large field, it can be tough to communicate the game start to both teams. In such a situation this method is useful: One team blows its whistle once when it is ready to go. The other team blows its whistle to signal "We heard you, and we're ready to go." The first team then blows its whistle a second time, which is the game-start signal. It works. (Leave the whistles at the flag stations in plain view so that when a team hangs the flag, the flag carrier blows that whistle to signal the game end.)

Length of Games

It depends. Listen to the rules. Generally, a game runs 20 minutes or until the flag is hung. Smaller groups might play 15-minute games. Special or scenario games can run for longer time (1, 2, 3, or more hours) or even for 24 hours continuously. Arenaball games might be only 3 or 5 minutes. Tournament five-man often is played as 10- or 12-minute games.

Paintgun Types

A game may be limited to a certain kind of paintgun. Most walk-on games (where you show up, and everyone is divided into two teams) are for semiautomatics powered by constant air (those

End-of-Game Signal

A game may be ended (as it started) with an audible, noisemaker signal (a whistle, bull horn, etc.). Usually the referees all call out "Game over! Barrel plugs in!" several times when the game is over, so everybody stops shooting. When hearing-impaired players are on the field, a visual end-of-game signal that works is for the refs (and even some players) to raise both hands overhead and wave them back and forth. All such signals need to be explained during the pregame orientation.

Who's the Ref?

The person in the striped shirt in red, blue, orange, white, hot pink, or yellow is the ref. Or maybe the person who has the whistle around her neck, or the one carrying the flags out to the stations is your ref. Just pay attention and you'll see who the refs are. A field may put its staff in matching shirts of a bright color that is easy to see and does not make the ref look like a player. Refs get shot often enough even when they are wearing bright yellow shirts.

Some few ref teams wear bright pants also, or an urban swat pattern, or blue jeans. They usually don't wear camouflage pants: to a player who's set down low, "camo" pants say "Bad guy!" and that leads to refs getting shot when they shouldn't.

Do not target-practice on the refs. They don't shoot back, but they can send you out of the game for shooting them deliberately. They can send you home, too.

Players on the field may be field refs enjoying a day off. They may, if needed, function as refs if a situation calls for it. Use common sense, and if someone in camo takes charge of a situation and appears to know what he or she is doing, don't be a jerk—do what the person says. For example, any time that anyone hears "Goggles! Stop shooting!" do it immediately because it means a person's goggles are not on. You don't need a red-shirted ref to make that kind of call.

Other Equipment on the Field

For walk-on games, smoke grenades sometimes are allowed, but usually not in dry areas. Paint grenades may be allowed. Walkie-talkies usually are allowed. Ghillie suits (the ones that make you look like Swamp Monster) are generally okay, as are costumes of various sorts as long as they don't interfere with safety. Tournaments, however, do not usually allow any of these.

What you can bring to the field depends on the local rules. Ask about pets, motor homes, overnight camping, and so forth. Smoking, barbecues, or cooking fires may be restricted to certain areas due to fire hazards.

Prohibited Behaviors

Don't use foul or abusive language, and don't get into arguments with players or refs. No aggressive physical contact with another person is tolerated. Drinking and paintball do not mix!

Questions and Gripes

Talk to the field staff, referees, field owner, or game organizer if you have a gripe or question. Written copies of the field's safety and playing rules should be posted, and often these are available in a pamphlet.

6

Take the Wire!

Positions to Play

"The Coach"

The basic areas of a paintball field are the two wires (the boundary tapes, left and right) and the center of the field. *Take the wire* means to position yourself along the left or the right wire (generally you will be pointed toward one or the other). You are supposed to pick a good spot and either hold or push up along the tape until you can go get the opposing team's flag. Which action you take will depend on what you run into on your wire.

A *point man* is the scout, the person who is out in front of the other players. Point men tend to be eliminated early in the game, so it's not necessarily a good spot for a new player who doesn't yet know the field or how to play the game. Against experienced players, Robbie Newbie as point person will usually head back to the staging area in short order.

Players on point must be alert.

A sniper looks for good ambush spots.

In thick brush, however, even a newbie point man can do well if he or she takes care to advance with all senses on alert. Whatever does not look like it belongs in the brush, probably doesn't.

A *sniper* is someone who goes out to a good ambush spot, hides, and waits for an unsuspecting opponent to come into range. Robbie Newbie, however, usually won't know what the good ambush spots are, since he won't know the field. Thus, it is hard for a newbie to play sniper unless the field is thick and there are many good sniper spots.

The *rover* is the player who has the keenest sense for what's happening all over the field. He or she uses eyes, ears, and that sixth sense (intuition) to sense which way the game is going. This is a very hard position to play. The rover has to

A rover has to understand the entire field situation.

react either to shore up a side that is falling or to join in with a side that is about to overpower the opponents. Sometimes the rover has to head home and defend the flag, or go solo through a zone that suddenly opens up. Newbies usually don't have the field sense to deal with all these options.

A *safety* is like a safety in football. It's your last hope to stop the opponents from scoring. A safety might be a lone defender. It might be a rover who reacts to a push and stops the push.

Robbie Newbie does not have to worry about all these names and positions. Understanding the wire concept is a good thing. When in doubt, if right-handed, go play the right wire. You know that there will not be any opponents off on your right, so you have less field to worry about being shot from.

Take the wire!

Twenty Tips for the New Player

James R. "Mad Dog" Morgan, Sr.

So you've just played your first day or two. And if your first day was anything like mine, you could sum it up by saying, "I came, I saw, I got spanked." You foolishly thought you had the necessary skills to take on the veterans in your first walk-on game. Well, now you know better. Does this describe the majority of your day? You were either outgunned, outranged, or outnumbered every time you stuck up your head so much as to look around.

You tried being aggressive, you tried laying back and defending. Let's face it, you tried everything you could think of—and still stopped more paintballs than the fattest tree on the field. You managed to find every booby trap and ambush spot on the field. You were lucky to survive one game, and if you took out a few opponents, you counted yourself amazed and knew it was not as many as you wished.

You must take heart. Over the many years I've been playing and writing about the game, I've become a rabid fanatic of the sport and an unflagging supporter of first-time and beginning players, so much so that I've been referred to as "King of the Newbies" (a title I retain with honor). As such, let me first shore up your bruised ego with some true stories of mistakes that I've made on the field. Sure, it's damaging to the ego, but, as many players will tell you, I've got plenty to spare.

Delusion

The first really stupid mistake on my first day was that, having come to the field the week before and witnessed a few games, I decided to try it for myself. So early that next Saturday, I got up and went to Canobie Paintball's indoor field in

Give your teammates help if they need it.

Canobie, New Hampshire (a field long since closed). They issued me a Razorback II pumpgun along with a JT Whipper Snapper goggle that smelled like my old junior high locker room.

I spent a few rounds at the target area. After hitting three targets in a row, I figured I'd have no problem doing some serious tail-kicking out there. Well, I was young back then, fast, wiry. I had been hunting on the family farm since I was 10, so I thought I had all the skills I needed. That delusion lasted approximately 30 seconds into the game.

Because, you see, one of my teammates warned me that some of our opposition played for a team called the New England Express. The name meant nothing to me at the time. I was so new to the sport that I was surprised to know that there even were teams, much less know about a world-champion-level team like the Express. All I knew about it was that the players weren't packing Razorback II pumps like us.

To make a long story short, I spent most of the first 30 seconds of the game watching as waves of

paint came in and annihilated most of my team-mates. Providence shined as I managed to make it into one of the buildings unscathed (probably by managing to run at a speed that was faster than the field limit). The last four minutes of the game consisted of my trying to clean out my barrel with one of those old foam "swab on a stick" squeegees while I cowered in the corner and listened to 15 paintballs a second hitting the building wall or just over my head.

Let's face it: I was toast just waiting to be buttered up.

As I awaited my doom, I heard the referee shout, "Hey! Take it easy on the Newbie!" And I, being me, naturally had to answer back, "Yeah, let me live five seconds longer than the normal idiot you talk into trying this game!"

Thus began the tradition of weird behavior and remarks that led to my becoming known as "The Mad Dog." That first day was painful, but nonetheless fun. I even got my first "kill" ("elim-

Leave quickly, with your arm up, when you are hit.

ination" for the Politically Correct among us). Let me tell that story.

My First One

About two games later, the referees had changed the teams around so that the Express players were on both teams. The refs had asked the Express to "tone down" the level of their play so we beginning players could get in on the fun. Well, I was part of a push down the left wall, and two of us had made it, still unpainted, into a hut at around midfield. Our main opposition was a player in the nearest hut on the other side of the field who had been proving himself quite accurate with that Tippmann 68 Special of his. He had thinned out our team by half.

Not knowing any better, we decided to go head to head with the guy. That lasted a good 15 seconds, until my partner took a goggle hit, leaving me all alone to face this serial painter. I got off a few shots that managed to hit his hut. Then our match degraded to a case of "woodchuck love" (you know, you pop up, shoot once, and duck down again; then your opponent does the same, and the cycle repeats itself for a while).

This fellow decided to stay up and wait for me to stick my head up from the same place I'd been stupidly popping up from for the last three minutes. True to form, up I came, right into his sights. A paintball whizzed within an inch of my ear. Reacting on pure instinct, I dodged so hard that I fell on my rear end. As a result of my attempt to maintain my balance, I pulled the trigger of my marker. As I was on my way to landing on my derrière, I watched my shot. It curved with the "English" of a Minnesota Fats cue ball and splattered in the middle of my antagonist's Realtree shirt. It would be a real contest to find out who was more surprised, him or me. But from that moment on, I was hooked on the sport.

When the game starts, have a plan.

How to Avoid Mistakes

As a new player, I tried to learn as much as I could from *Action Pursuit Games* and other magazines. It helped, but the magazines don't cover everything you could possibly do wrong. As you might figure, even now I keep making up new "rules" to prevent my making more mistakes on the field. Here are some of them:

1. You should take the barrel plug out of your 'gun *before* you have someone "dead to rights" in your sights.
2. Sticking your head up in the same place more than twice transforms you from a paintball player into the main attraction at a turkey shoot.
3. When you've set up that perfect ambush and have two players just walking into it, it's a good idea not to have a watch that "beeps" on the hour.

4. Never shoot at sounds going through the bushes. Your fellow teammates and referees make noises, too.
5. Remember which color armband you have on. And try to remember it's the members of the *other* team you're supposed to eliminate.
6. Never forget you have peripheral vision. You see a player (sometimes it's even a teammate) and become so engrossed with eliminating him that you don't realize there are other guys around until one sticks his barrel practically into your side.

Hold your fire when opponents are in the next zip code.

Refillable air tanks provide a constant air source.

Keep your loader full so you don't run dry.

7. If you're not defending the flag or waiting in ambush, never stay in the same place too long—or all you've done is pick your grave site.

8. Let your teammates know where you are. Friends are nice to have. Friendly fire isn't.

9. Talk to your teammates, and let them know what's happening—or the only words you'll be saying are "Ouch, ouch, ow, hit. Hit! Out!"

10. Give your teammates help if they need it, or ask for help if you need it. Even a mediocre team is better than a good individual player.

11. Don't shoot at someone when you see he's in the next zip code. If you freeze in place, he'll most likely not see you until he's so close that you can't miss.

12. Watch your backside. I mean, be careful it doesn't stick out from behind cover. It's by far everyone's favorite target.

13. Be sure to check out what team a player is on before taking orders from him.

14. On the first game of the day be a bit more careful before entering a hut. Sometimes they're occupied by unwelcome guests. And from personal experience, it is true that skunks are faster on the draw than the average paintballer.

Vary your tactics so you're not predictable.

15. No matter how great the location seems, poison ivy, poison oak, and ragweed patches are not good brush to hide in.

16. Lace your shoes very tightly on fields with marshes. Many a shoe has never been recovered from certain fields. It is just rumor, however, that in some marshes all that has been found was an occasional hand holding up an autowhat-ever from the muck.

17. Don't go out onto the field late in the day unless you're sure you've got more gas in the bottle than you've got from the field food.

You don't have to shoot what you can outwit.

18. Never use the same tactic exclusively. Being tagged as "Ol' Reliable" is not a compliment.

19. Never take a player "head on" unless you have to. It's fine for John Wayne, but he has a stunt double, background music, and a script that says the other guy is going down. Always try to get around and behind an opponent who's dug into a defensive position.

20. Always know just about how much paint you have left in your loader, and never let it run dry. They always rush you as you reload.

Shoot Backward

Now I'll have to relate some of the really stupid mistakes I've discovered over the years. For instance, let's say you're the General in a Big Game. Say you've had a ball break in your Auto-cocker and you have just "squeegeed" it out. Do you know what happens if you are in such a hurry to shoot back that you forget to put the bolt back in? The 'gun can "shoot backward," taking out You, the General. (Yes, I "killed myself.")

No one who knows me from back when I was just getting started will forgive me if I don't tell the story of my Ultimate Oops. It's definitely one for the books, which I hear time and again around the campfires of old paintball cartons.

Once upon a time, I tried to sneak through the swamp-bridge field at Adventure Games of New Hampshire. In the previous game on one side of this field, I had managed to sneak through heavy brush and cattails, get behind the opposition, and do some really great backshooting. I was high on adrenaline and felt that I was invincible, so I figured I'd just go do the same thing on the other side of the field.

The game started off okay. I moved right and with little trouble sneaked to the bunker known as "Firebase Gloria." Between Firebase Gloria and the other side of the field was a small meadow covered in waist-deep grass and a few fallen trees. I figured I'd have my best chance to get across by doing a Marine belly crawl, so on my belly I went, disregarding the muck and mud. I moved very slowly, listening all the time for the rustle of grass or branches that would have meant that an enemy player was lying in wait for me. I got two-thirds of the way across and heard a rustle. It was very close.

"Somebody knows I'm here and is trying to find me! He hasn't shot yet, so he doesn't know exactly where I am. It's a case of whoever finds the other first!" I thought.

Slowly, cautiously, I spent the next 10 minutes slowly using my scope to examine every leaf and blade of grass out there. Then I spotted him. He was 20 feet away and looking right at me, but it didn't matter.

He was only seven inches tall.

Boy, did I feel stupid. I, Mad Dog, had been held at bay for 15 minutes by an unarmed chipmunk. It was years before I lived that down. My teammates would constantly remind me to "beware of the killer chipmunk" every time I went on that field.

Mistake-Free

Now, can any of your tactical mistakes compare to that? Yeah, sure, you made those mistakes and

Use peripheral vision, and keep looking around.

your pride got hurt, and so did your ego. But if you learn from your mistakes as I did, you will become a better player for it. My string of mistakes was practically a legend for a time, but now few people want to take me on without help. I've been giving out many more "Mad Dog Got You" buttons than "Mad Dog's Death Certificates" for quite a while.

Paintball is a game where everyone can improve and become a great player. Everyone competes in this sport on equal grounds, and I haven't heard of that in any other games this side of Monopoly. Yes, a few people will have a natural aptitude for the game, but everyone else, even those veterans out there who just choose to forget they once were Robbie Newbies themselves, came up the same way you did. They played, made some mistakes, learned from the mistakes, and got better and better.

Having sufficiently damaged my reputation and ego for a while, let me give you my last observation. I may not have done every stupid thing possible on a paintball field (not for want of circumstances), and I know some of you out there have stories that compare with my exploits. But most stupid mistakes are survivable and bruise only our egos, and if we only do something stupid once in a while, it just proves that we're still human.

To prevent you from making the one really stupid mistake that you never want to make in paintball: *Keep your goggles on!*

How to Learn the Game

1. Use your brain more than your trigger finger. Paintball is a mental game as much as a physical one. You don't have to outshoot a player you can outwit.

2. Keep your eyes and ears open at all times. A good sense of situational awareness is a great asset. It's a darn fact that when you focus your attention on any one area during a game, the paintball that eliminates you will come from another direction.

3. The most pain(t)less way to learn is to watch other players. Good players will use tactics you want to copy, and bad players will make goofs you don't want to repeat. It's a lot less damaging to the ego if you learn from the mistakes the other guys make, without having to make them yourself.

4. Learn to balance aggression with caution. Keep close enough to get into the action, and be able to retreat without exposing yourself too greatly.

5. Most important, this is a game. You're not here to collect scalps. You're here to have fun.

Ten Key Pointers for Newbies

Jim "Roadrunner" Fox

Paintball schools aren't much in the picture yet in this sport. New players, newbies, hunger for information about the game and want to learn how to play better. Here's a set of things a newbie can work on, week after week, to become a better player. Ponder the points slowly during the week. Remember what you did the week before as you revisit these concepts. Practice, practice, practice. You'll become a better player for it.

1. Field of Vision

A newbie's field of vision will not be as good as that of an experienced player. To play well you need to look deep and long into areas, not just for players' bodies and parts thereof, but also for equipment, such as paintgun barrels, hoppers, loaders, and large constant-air tanks. Also look for

Look deeper into the brush for hidden players.

propellant being expelled, paintballs flying out from a position, and foliage moving. You might see only a silhouette of a body, or shadowy figures, or quick flashes of something moving fast.

At first, your ability to look deep into the field and find visuals will not be very good. You won't see far at all. Keep looking from side to side, so nobody can flank you. Look behind also. Concentrate on finding the opposition. Then you can work on tagging them out.

Aim before you pull the trigger.

2. Aim!

Aiming is the key to success. Newbies are not the only ones who "just shoot," but they do it more frequently than do more experienced players. Yes, it's hard to aim with eye protection on, but you must protect your eyes.

You can aim a paintgun in different ways. Use the sight rails. Try red dot or lighted sights. Just look down the barrel, especially if you have a power feed. Whatever way you aim your paintgun is better than simply shooting it without taking aim. If you just shoot at someone, chances are you will miss. Aim. Then shoot. Your chances of getting an elimination will drastically increase.

3. Shoot!

Not shooting is one of the reasons newbies evolve slowly in this sport. Newbies don't shoot during a paintball game because they don't want to give away their position. Well, chances are, they were seen already, unless the newbie players crawled into really thick brush. Another reason newbies don't shoot is that they think if they open up on someone, they will be hit by return fire. This isn't always the case. Players miss; players don't see opponents shoot all of the time.

Newbies feel the longer they stay untagged in a game, the better it looks for them. This is not true. Players look up to other players who make great moves, get the pull and hang, take out the opposition, or assist a teammate with needed cover-fire. The final reason newbies don't shoot enough is money. Newbies more than likely do not have a lot of money to buy a case of paint every time out. This is understandable, but shooting and eliminating your opponents is half the fun and a much needed part of the game.

Take your shots in moderation. If you use a pump, shoot once every three or four seconds unless you need to shoot faster. If you use a semi, shoot in two- or three-round bursts to conserve paint. Also shoot at your opponents, not at the protection they are hidden behind. Shoot to the side of the tree the opponent is hiding behind. Your paint is not going to go through that tree! And remember that you can effectively keep an opponent pinned down with conservative shots just as well as with rapid fire.

4. Judge Distances

Develop a sense of the distance between you and your target. You need to know estimated distances from one point to another. Then you need to know how far paintballs will fly—and how far they fly accurately. With experience you will be able to determine just how far away an opponent is in relation to you and or a teammate, which will give you a better sense of what moves you can make. Learn to measure in yards (or meters), not feet. Yardage and meters are easier to figure out. Your yardage will be off at first, but just keep working at it.

Look for good cover.

5. Good Cover

Teaching about cover is probably one of the most important pieces of advice a player shares with another. As a newbie you need to know how to use only the best of cover. Whether you are standing, kneeling, or lying down behind something, make sure the cover is large enough for your entire body. New players seem to think that if they are behind something they will not be detected by anyone (and that incoming paintballs therefore will not hit them). This is not true. Get behind something that gives you protection in front and to each side of you.

Try to pick your cover before you go into it. Do not try to get in with someone else when there is only room for one person. Make sure your body position conforms to the configuration of your cover. For example, don't stand behind a big, wide rock that only comes up chest high. Get down on your knees and look up over the rock and around each of its sides.

6. Communicate

Without communication you have no teamwork. Without teamwork, you and your teammates will not win. Giving and receiving information makes it easier to pinpoint targets and get flag pulls and hangs. It helps coordinate maneuvers and gives a novice player a sense of security.

Communicate to your teammates where and how many of the opposition you see. Tell them if your paintgun is down or if you need paint. Tell them when you are being pinned down and ask for cover-fire. Know how much time has elapsed. Except the person waiting to ambush or a low crawler, everyone on the team should talk it up during a game. These ambush and crawling players cannot speak, but, nevertheless, you must relay information to them.

7. Partner Up

Get yourself an experienced player who will assist you during the games you play. He or she can tell you what you should or should not do. An experienced player's field of vision is a lot better than a newbie's. He or she can help a newbie decide

Buddy up with an experienced player.

Watch your flanks.

what is suitable cover and provide an abundance of cover-fire, and has better game timing.

An experienced player can assist if you have trouble with your paintgun or need paint. You will learn a lot when you partner up with someone who has more experience. Before you know it, you will be partnering up with a newbie. *You* will be the experienced player doing the teaching.

8. Movement

When players move during a game, they are hard to hit. If you stay in one spot for a long time, you will eventually be found, sweet-spotted, and more than likely eliminated. Move around. Try to find better cover and angles from which to shoot at your opponents.

Move to confuse your opposition. Move to get a better look at something or at different parts of the field. Remember, a moving target is much harder to hit than a stationary one. Move defensively when an opponent sees or shoots at

you. Run or dive for cover (if you are out in the open). Drop straight to the ground.

Move in various ways. You can, of course, run, walk, jog, leap, and so on. You can also crawl or duckwalk if you need to. Move your body out

Move around unless you are setting up an ambush.

Work in pairs to get angle shots.

of the line of incoming paintballs. Move forward or backward when your teammates do.

9. Adjust Shots

A player must know how to correct shots when shooting at a specific target. When a player pulls up to shoot at someone or someplace, he or she usually does not need to adjust from side to side. It is the vertical height that mostly needs to be adjusted.

Arc your paintballs in on players who are far away. Learn to "walk-in" your shots. You can either start low and keep coming up until you are on target, or you can start high and then bring your paintgun down. Aim for whatever your opponent gives you to shoot at. If you have a full-body shot, aim for the center mass (the chest area).

10. Angles

Shooting angles is what every player strives for. To get an angle on a player's right or left side, you must move right or left, or flank them, while your opponent remains at his original position. What this does is expose more of your opponent's body, making him a bigger target. This is called "slicing the pie." Cut a little bit more off the pie every time, and eventually you'll get that last slice and send your opponent off the field.

Make sure you have sufficient cover when moving right or left. Watch so your opponents don't get the angle on you. Opponents will concentrate their fire on you from two, three, or more positions. If this happens, get support from your teammates and retreat. Keep your team on a line so the other team can't get around on one side of you. If you see a player start to move to flank you, move laterally with him so he won't be able to get the angle on you.

Every player in this sport will benefit from working on the basics all the time. Practice, keep playing, and continue learning. When you can apply something that you have learned here, you'll be thankful for the hours you spent thinking your way to success.

How to Plan a Private Game

Richard Dufault

So, you've heard of paintball, or perhaps you've played a couple of times. You want to go again, but no one is organizing a game. Why not do it yourself? With a little work and good planning, you can set up a game for you and your friends or co-workers.

The "nuts and bolts" of organizing a game will keep you busy. The first time is the toughest because there are lots of details to take care of. After organizing your first game, it gets much easier. Yes, organizing a private game will take some time, but it's fun.

Who Are You?

What type of group do you have? Are you just getting friends to come out together and play paintball? Are you organizing a game for your office crowd? Do you work for a retail chain, with lots

of potential players? How you plan for the day is affected by who's going to participate.

Planning for the event means less pressure if it's a game with your friends. With officemates, things need to go well. After all, you work with these folks all week long, so having a good time can have wonderful long-term results on your life five out of seven days of every week.

On the other hand, with a private game for co-workers it may be easier to take care of the financial end, especially if you're organizing the game in conjunction with your Human Resources or Special Events department. Bonus: It's fun to "put paint" on a boss.

Afterward

As you plan the day, you might want to organize an after-game event, so everyone can enjoy a cool

Good planning + good attitudes = good time

refresher and some spicy finger food while they reminisce about their glorious day. After all, the only thing more fun than playing paintball is telling stories about it afterward. You can ask the field owner if there is a place he or she might recommend that is not too far away. Remind everyone to bring a change of clothes, and choose a place with an atmosphere that welcomes a sports team coming in after a game.

Money

Find out how much it will cost each player for the greens fee, a reasonable amount of paint, rental gear, camouflage, and any extras for the event. Most fields offer package deals and group rates. When collecting the money ahead of time, always give receipts, even when dealing with friends; nothing can ruin a friendship faster than money problems on the day of the game. Never use your own money to pay for someone who will "pay you back later" because if they don't pay you back or

they don't show up to play, there will be friction in your friendship.

Ask if the field uses the concept of non-refundable deposit, which is fine. After all, the field owner can't run a business where he's expected to get ready, hire referees and support staff, and buy food and paintballs only to find out half your group did not show up and hear "Can't we have our money back?" Let your group know that if they don't show, there's no refund. You can sometimes use substitute players; you just collect the money from them to give back to the person who didn't show up. Take care about who you allow into your game, though.

When talking to your friends about paintball, tell them up front how much it will cost. This is important so that your friends will understand that paintball is not cheap. If the office is paying, you'll need a good estimate of how much the whole day will cost. Bosses don't like surprise bills, so do not underestimate costs. The field owner should be able to give you a good idea of total costs, having been through this many times.

The Package

Package deals for groups vary from field to field. Always insist the package include goggles with full head-protection systems and a paintgun with loader, assuming your players do not have their own gear. If needed, see that the package also includes jumpsuits or camouflage jackets and pants (these protect well from the bushes), and belts and pouches to hold ammo.

What kind of paintguns should you rent? The basic choices are stockguns, pumpguns, and semi-automatics. With new players, any of these work.

Camouflage can be rented at most paintball fields.

The field has rental headgear and markers and sells paintballs.

The cost for renting semiautos is usually higher. And you're likely to shoot more paint with a semi, meaning more money is required. Whatever you choose, the whole group should have the same kind of 'gun. Stock- and pumpguns use less paint (lower costs) and your players will not get hit as many times. They do require a bit of coordination to use. You have to pump the 'gun once each time you want to get a paintball into the chamber so you can shoot it. Semiautomatics are easier to learn for people who aren't used to shooting pump-style 'guns. You fill the loader with paint, cock the 'gun once, and it recocks itself after each shot. Only one paintball is shot with each trigger pull, as with a stockgun or pumpgun.

Ask what else is available that costs extra. This might include lunch, paint or smoke grenades, refills on your CO_2 or compressed-air tanks, and photos of your group. One great way to save money is to purchase paintballs by the case. Cases usually come packaged with 1,000, 2,000 or 2,500 paintballs to the case. Most fields sell partial cases, too.

How many games will you play? This depends on how long you will be playing and how fast your group "turns around" between games.

Organizing groups and bringing them out to the field is a lot of work. Often a field will not charge the organizer himself or will offer some other goodies as a "thank you" for the efforts. This is something the field owner should tell you about as you work on getting the group together. It's not impolite to ask about this. Larger fields have contracts with booking agents and travel agencies who bring groups on a regular basis.

Field Choices

Call around to the fields in your area and compare prices. Visit each field and look at the facilities. One might have a pro shop and picnic tables or covered areas where you can have lunch out of the sun. Another might have just woods and a check-in stand. These all affect what price you're willing to pay for the day.

Ask whether the field has liability insurance, and ask for the name of the carrier. Some companies will want this information before taking a group out to play.

You might want to confirm your research by visiting the fields whose owners you've called. You can visit several fields in one day, assuming you have lots of fields in your area. It's best to go when the field is having games so you can see how they operate. Call ahead the day before to get permission and directions, and go out there!

Ask if you can visit the playing fields with a referee or staff member. They'll generally have you sign a waiver and lend you an orange vest (to identify you as an observer) and goggles. Check out the sanitary facilities and see whether they are kept clean. Ask players on the scene if they are having fun. Count how many referees are on hand: There should never be fewer than one ref for each 15 to 20 or so players, and never fewer than two refs on a field, even for a small game of five on five.

Look for safety signs, and make sure the staff enforce safety rules. Do they enforce barrel-plug usage? Do they use chronographs? These devices check how fast a paintball is leaving the 'gun. There are maximum speed limits used worldwide. Are the rental goggles' lenses clear (not all scratched up and dull)? Use your good judgment. Safety comes first. Friendly field staff and good equipment will help make the day a pleasure.

No Sharks!

You're organizing a private game. That means you don't want outsiders in the game if you can prevent it. However, suppose the field requires a minimum number of players for the game, and you're short (a couple of folks didn't show up). Should you pick up outsiders to fill the rosters or just pay the fees for the no-shows and keep the game private?

Is your group made up of players new to the game? Sharks and minnows should never swim in the same pond. Newbies (minnows) shouldn't share the same field with experienced players (sharks) unless some strict ground rules have first been laid down. With newbies, you don't want outside sharks in the game. A shark may be a pro (tournament) player, a "home team" player, or anyone you don't know who has his own gear. All it might take to ruin everyone's day are a couple of sharks splattering your buddies with scads of paint. You must *never* let sharks play as a team against your team of minnows, no matter how much smaller the shark group might be. You are just asking to be painted up, and you won't have much fun.

Not all experienced players are jerks. There are well-equipped players who take the time to talk to beginners, show them how to play, and let them examine or use their expensive equipment. These nice people might not be bad to play with. But why take a chance? You may only play paintball once or twice this year, and you don't want a bad day to waste your hard-earned money.

Spend time at the target range before games begin.

Keep your game private if you can. Ask the field owner how many you must bring to avoid being put into a walk-on game (that's a game with everyone who isn't with a group, including whatever sharks are there to play). Usually you must have 15 to 20 prepaid players to ensure having a private game.

Think Ahead

You'll have plenty to think about in planning the day. The best preparation is for you to go play paintball as a walk-on at least a month before your group goes out to play. That will give you some experience and help you to plan.

A big question to consider before the playing day is this: How will you choose sides, and what will you do if one side keeps winning every game? Just remember, however much fun it is to be on the winning side all day, it isn't fun when you are on the losing side all day. Our recreational group, the Boggie Peril, uses the patented Boggie Tradition to make sure everyone gets to win during the day. We switch members between teams every two games, and we try to make sure the teams are even before we head to the fields. We allow buddies to stay together if that is their wish.

Another big question is what to wear. Ask the field owner if there will be water (creeks), mud, hills, or sand, and choose footwear accordingly. Cover that skin! Paintballs are firm, little gelatin capsules that can sting when they hit you, and they can leave bruises. Both drawbacks are emphasized if a paintball hits bare skin. Long sleeves and long pants are a must. If you rent coveralls (jumpsuits), wear shorts and a T-shirt underneath.

Gloves are good to wear.

If you own fingerless gloves and don't mind getting them painted, by all means bring them, too. Garden gloves (the two-dollar kind) are good; cut the glove fingers off so the first two finger joints are not covered. If you own knee pads, wear them. Bring a baseball hat. You can wear it backward with your goggles. The hat will keep paintballs and the sun off your head, and the bill will protect the back of your neck in case you get shot from behind. For cold-weather play, wear many layers so you can peel off excess layers when the going gets hot—and trust me, it will!

Bring water, plenty of it, and something to eat if you're not partaking of the lunch offered at the field. Leave alcohol at home. Drinking and paintguns do not mix.

To help your group know what to do and how the game is played, it's good to have a meeting with a question-and-answer session at least a week before the game. That gives them plenty of time to get things together for the day. Pass out maps to the field and the field phone number in case anyone gets lost. Carpool or caravan if possible.

Long pants and long sleeves are recommended.

No Whiners!

The world is full of whiners and crybabies. Remember that before you head out to the field. Paintball is a sport that involves shooting your opponents. Some egos will be bruised, and bodies will get lumps and bumps that go with the game. Attitude, therefore, is important. It's your responsibility as organizer to make sure to hear any complaints and deal with them. If some of your group have complaints about safety or other field operations, see the field owner or manager immediately. Safety comes first, and after that you want everyone to have a good time so they'll want to play in your next game. If safety is an issue at that field, leave and never return.

Best Time

With good planning, good choices, and good attitudes, you and your friends should have just about the best time you've ever had. You'll know you had a good time when you finally get home, plop down on the couch, and start to think of the next time. Yup, next time that sneaky so-and-so won't get the drop on you, no sirree!

And the planning begins again. . . .

Paintball builds office teamwork.

For Parents Only

Joshua Flynn

Many people have heard of paintball and have developed stereotypes of the sport. Some people say that paintball is dangerous and disruptive to our youth. This could not be further from the truth. In reality, paintball is a lot safer than most other sports and it teaches many valuable morals.

First of all, let's look at the misconception that paintball is a dangerous sport. This is terribly wrong. The truth is, far more injuries occur in football or soccer than in paintball. One of the reasons for this is that the rules of paintball forbid physical contact. In football, physical contact is a vital part of the game. In soccer, there are times when two or more players collide, causing injuries. This does not happen in paintball because players tag each other from a distance.

Paintball also is a good way for people to learn some good basic skills, such as teamwork, problem solving, and social skills.

No generation gap: father and son

Teamwork

It is important that you have good teamwork skills when playing paintball. If you don't work as a unit with the other members of your team, you will not succeed. Paintball teaches this concept to kids, adults, and even business corporations. Many businesses schedule paintball outings just to build teamwork skills.

William Foody receives the "In Search of Excellence" award from Debra Krischke at the 2000 Zap International Amateur Open.

Young guns at the 2000 Zap International Amateur Open

Problem Solving

You learn problem-solving techniques in paintball. The objective in paintball is to capture the opposing team's flag and return it to your home base—without getting marked or tagged by a paintball. Along the way to capturing the flag, you are likely to encounter problems. You may be outnumbered, have 'gun problems, or have your own flag captured. You must come up with a way to overcome these misfortunes. This concept is known as problem solving and is valuable in everyday life.

Social Skills

Paintball also can help younger players develop social skills. Many youngsters have trouble talk-

ing to adults about problems they are having. Sometimes they are embarrassed to talk about something because they think adults will think it is stupid.

Young guns learn paintgun technology.

When you play paintball you are constantly talking to other people on your team. If someone has problems with their 'gun, there are usually adults who will be more than happy to help them out. Adults on the field work with younger players, encouraging them to become better players and constantly giving them helpful ideas to help them improve. When young players interact with adults in positive ways, they overcome their fears and develop good social skills that they can use in life—the real world.

As you can see, paintball is not the "terrible war game" some make it out to be. By incorporating real life skills into a fast-paced game, paintball can be a good influence for anyone. It's a great way to build many skills that can be taken from the paintball field and carried to the real playing field of life.

Mature young players can compete equally with adults.

Let the Games Begin

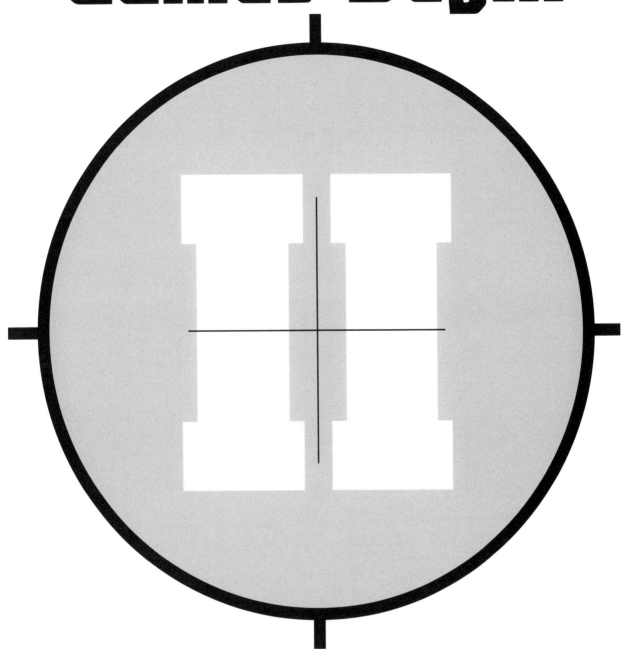

A Baker's Dozen Games

Jim "Roadrunner" Fox

Paintball usually is played as a two-team, Capture the Flag game. That's not the only way to play, though, and the Roadrunner has put together this list of other options you might want to try. These are time-tested and lots of fun!

Capture the Flag

The most popular and most widely used game format in paintball is called Capture the Flag. This format is used extensively everywhere paintball is played: recreational play sites, clubs, and on the tournament circuit.

Capture the Flag can be played indoors or outdoors. Players are divided into teams, usually two. Each team has a starting point (flag station) and a flag at that station. To win the game, your team

Capture the flag from your opponent's flag station and take it to your own flag station to win the game.

must go and capture the opposing team's flag and bring it back to your flag station. The suggested game time is 15 minutes for games with a few new players on small fields and 20 minutes for games with more players. Really big games (more than

50 players on a side) can last longer. In all paint-ball games the suggested time limits are optional. They often depend on the size of the field, the skill level of the players, and the number of players in the game. Shorter games are usually better because more of them can be played.

Rules

All play-site operators have rules of play they prefer to use. When you go to a play site, these rules will be explained during orientation. That's a time before the games start when the staff explains the play and safety rules and answers questions. The rules will be slightly different everywhere you play, so listen closely at orientation and don't hesitate to ask about what you don't understand.

The rules of the game affect how you play. For example, there are always rules concerning the flag. The flag runner usually must carry the flag in plain view at all times. If the flag carrier is tagged out, any other player on his team can take the flag from him and try to advance it (*live-flag* rule). Sometimes, the flag carrier who is tagged has to take the flag all the way back to the opposing team's flag station before it can be advanced again (*dead-flag* rule).

An exciting part of the game is trying to tag your opponents out of the game. If you put a splat mark on an opponent, he or she has to leave the game (score a personal victory for you!). Deciding how a player is eliminated always requires a few rules. Nearly everywhere, a player is tagged out of the game when marked with a splat of paint the size of a quarter or larger. If a paintball bounces off a player, the player is still in the game. If the paintball splats on something besides the player and puts paint spray on the player, it is called splatter. Splatter does not eliminate a player under nearly all rules unless the splatter is the size of a quarter or larger.

Tactics

With few players on each team, say 10, the basic strategy sends all your players out on offense and leaves no defense. To leave a defense weakens your attacking team by a large percentage. Leaving 1 of 10 on defense weakens your attack by 10 percent. If the other team gets to your flag station, chances are you will have reached their flag station as well, and you can adjust your game plan according to how many players you have left after you've captured the opponents' flag. With larger teams, you can leave one, two, or more players back on defense.

Since paintball is a *living* video game, you cannot predict how each game will play out. The players on each team usually form into small groups (squads). Some will play alone. Each team has a general overall game plan, and each squad gets sent into one zone (area of the field) with the assignment of attacking aggressively (offense) or perhaps being a blocking squad. The tactics a team chooses will vary from game to game, and it is up to the team and its players how they go about playing the game.

Arenaball

Arenaball is paintball played in an arena, with spectators. This game is also called speedball. The arena should be about 60 yards or meters by 40 yards or meters. Some structures are okay but nothing should keep the spectators from seeing the action. Structures should be high and narrow, so players stay on their feet. Low structures tend to create boring games, with players on their knees, trying to hide, rather than up and moving.

Rules

Arenaball is for fast, quick action. Team sizes of some three to seven players are about right. The game time is 5 to 10 minutes. The game can be played as Capture the Flag with two flags, football, or elimination. It can be played with each player having only a limited amount of paint, say 100 or 200 paintballs or less.

Tactics

Arenaball games go quickly. When you have more players than your opponents, you have a two-on-one match-up somewhere on the field, and your team should take advantage of this.

Attack and Defend

This variation of Capture the Flag has one flag in one flag station defended by one team. The other team has no flag station and no flag to defend. Its members simply attack. The attacking team wins the game if they capture the flag and remove it a certain distance from the flag station.

Rules

Attack and Defend has rules similar to those for Capture the Flag. Suggested game time for fewer than 10 players is 10 minutes. For 10 to 40 players,

the game continues for 20 minutes. Larger groups can play longer games.

Tactics

In Attack and Defend the attacking team wants to get as many angles on the defenders as possible. Surrounding the flag station usually is a good tactic. Under some rules, the defenders can go out from their flag station, which makes the game still more interesting.

Football

This variation of the paintball game has one flag only, set in the middle of the playing field. Each team starts equidistant from the flag. The object of the game is to capture the flag and advance it through the opposing team until you can put the flag in a designated place, like a flag station. It's like moving the football through your opponents and across the goal line they are defending.

Rules

Football has the same rules as Capture the Flag. A variation of this game asks your team to only capture the flag and hold it (not lose possession) until a set amount of time has expired. A suggested game time is from 10 to 20 minutes. These Football game variants are often used at the end of the day when there are fewer players left.

Tactics

Many teams choose one or two flag grabbers before the game starts. They might even put down their

In Attack and Defend, attackers should surround the defenders' base.

paintguns and just run for the flag. If one player grabs the flag, he can bring it back where the rest of the team has set up. Then the team regroups and tries to advance it again. This tactic does not work in a game where you cannot go backward with the flag, a variation of the rules. After the team regroups, the team advances and eliminates opponents as best it can until the flag can be hung.

Elimination

Another popular form of Capture the Flag is called Elimination. It is a very simple game. Each team tries to eliminate all the rest of the other team by tagging them out with paintballs. The team that loses all its players first loses the game.

Rules

Use a short time limit, 5 to 10 minutes, as Elimination is usually played when there are only a few players, such as at the end of the day.

Tactics

The tactics here are to get at least two of your teammates playing against only one opponent. The two should be able to get angles on the one player and tag him or her out. Then the two move on to the next opponent.

Top Gun

At the end of the day, a variation of Elimination puts all players on the field in different spots. The object of the game is to be the last player not eliminated. The winner is the Top Gun.

Rules

Restrict the time to only 5 or 10 minutes of play.

Tactics

Some players wait until they see two players shooting at each other. Then they sneak up on one or the other and get an easy tag. Others hide and let players eliminate each other, and then come out of hiding and see what they can do.

Fox and Hounds

Still another variation of Elimination, also called Hounds and the Rabbit, calls for two or three

When you are the Fox, you get a head start from the Hounds.

match since it is so outnumbered. The Hounds will want to spread out until they make contact with a Fox, and then have players team up to eliminate that Fox before looking for the next Fox. It is also important for the Hounds to communicate so they know when they have found all the Fox team members.

Predator

A variation of Fox and Hounds turns every player eliminated by a Fox team member into a Fox team member. In other words, when a Hound is tagged, he becomes a Fox—and the Fox team grows.

Rules

The second time anyone on the Fox team is tagged, he or she is out of the game. The two-tags rule applies to the original Fox team members so they can stay in until tagged twice, too. This game can run until all the Hounds have become Fox-team members.

Tactics

The Fox team wants recruits as quickly as possible, and so it will want to plan accordingly. Again, circling back to the flag station undetected gives them a good chance to pick up some new team members unexpectedly.

Pink

This variation of Capture the Flag starts out with two regular teams each wearing different col-

players to be chased by the rest of the players. Typically the Fox team (or the Rabbit team) gets a head start and leaves the flag station before the rest of the players. Its members usually are more advanced players to make the game challenging to both teams. The Fox team wins if it eliminates all the Hounds, and the Hounds win if they tag out all the Fox team.

Rules

Set the time limit at 15 to 20 minutes.

Tactics

The Fox team may want to circle undetected and ambush the Hounds near the flag station. The Fox team often goes to thick brush, where it is hard to find them, and sets up an ambush. It is hard for the Fox team to win in a heads-up paint-slinging ored armbands. Each team has a flag station and a flag to defend, and the goal of capturing and hanging the opposing team's flag. Two players wear pink armbands (a color not worn by the other two teams). When the game starts, the Pinks can be anywhere on the field. They get a head start.

Every player on either team who is tagged by a Pink goes off the field and gets a pink armband, and comes back in the game. The Pink team tries to capture either flag and hang it on the opposite flag station. Pink does not have its own flag station. Any one of the three teams can win the game by capturing and hanging the flag.

Rules

The first time each of the two original Pink team members is tagged, he or she gets to go off the field and then come back in again. The other Pink team members are eliminated when tagged. The suggested game time is 20 minutes if there are fewer than 40 players, and 35 minutes if there are more.

Tactics

The two regular teams need to capture the flag as quickly as possible because their numbers will go down as more and more of them become Pinks. When the Pink team gets strong, it will be able to capture either flag and win the game because the two regular teams will have been weakened. The two original Pinks may want to set an ambush for one team and tag as many players as possible, because even if the two of them are tagged, they will get to come back into the game with all the players they just tagged.

Cutthroat

This tournament-style version of paintball puts multiple teams on the field at the same time. Each has a starting position (flag station). Teams are usually no larger than seven players. The object of the game is to eliminate as many other players as possible. The game also can be played with flags (either one per team or one per team plus bonus flags placed at different spots on the field).

Each player has a number. For example, the players on Team 1 will be 11, 12, 13, and 14 for a four-player team. When Player 14 tags out Player 44, the referee records the information. After the game ends, the referees tally the number of eliminations each team scored collectively. If flags are used, the points for flag captures are also tallied. Several games are played, usually at least five, and the teams finish for the day according to how many points have been scored.

Rules

Teams rotate starting positions by jumping two or three spaces each game. For example, Team 1 starts at position 1 in game 1, but it starts in position 3 for game 2 (jumps two spots). This rotation keeps a player from being next to the same teams at the start of every game. A typical game time for 10 different teams would be 30 minutes.

Tactics

Your team can stay together or split up. You might go after a weaker team that starts near you. Or you might want to run as fast as possible to another spot on the field if you are starting between two

Whatever the game, shoot straight.

Rules

Ten Shot games are usually only three to five minutes long. If you play with 12-gram paintguns, each player is allowed only one or two 12-grams. Under some rules you may pick paint up off the ground if you find any that is worth putting in your paintgun.

The amount of paint each player carries in One Shot may be limited to 10 or 20 paintballs, or it may be unlimited. The suggested time limit is 10 minutes for 10 players; continue longer for more players.

Tactics

In Ten Shot, it's simple: Don't miss, aim!

The trick to playing good One Shot is to have easy access to your paintballs. Keep them loose in your pocket, but watch that you don't break them if you crawl, jump, or bump around. Keep three or four paintballs in your hand. Knowing how to use your paintgun will help a lot, no matter whether you have a semiautomatic or a simple stockgun. Make every shot count. Aim! When you play in other formats, players don't aim all of the time.

very strong teams. The tactics will vary according to your position and the field terrain, your opponents, and your need to score points.

Ten Shot and One Shot

Ten Shot can be played in any format. It usually is played when there are no more than 10 players per side. Each player gets only 10 paintballs to shoot. A variation of this game is Twelve Shot (12 paintballs only). The winner is the team with the most players left at the end of the game.

One Shot, a variation on Ten Shot, does not allow any player to have any kind of bulk loader, tube, or stick feeder. Each paintball must be dropped into the paintgun one at a time.

Tag Up (Reincarnation)

This variation of any game lets a player who is eliminated go back to his flag station or to a designated spot and tag up. He cleans off the splatter mark. Then the player gets to go back into the game. A variation of this game called Penalty Box makes the player wait for one to five minutes before going back into the game.

Stick with your buddies in Big Games.

In Big Games that run continuously for several hours, a player may wait for five minutes or longer before being allowed back into the game. Football makes a good game to use with Tag Up.

Rules

Time limit is 20 to 35 minutes. A player can get more paint or CO_2 anytime he is tagged out, and players can stop playing anytime they wish. If a team wins the game, start another one. Referees must pay attention: If one team's home base gets pretty well surrounded, the game should be stopped, because players tagging up are just going to get hit again (not fun).

Tactics

Just have fun! You're going to come back into the game fairly quickly under most versions of this game, so don't worry about getting tagged. Play hard and shoot a lot of paint.

Big Game

A Big Game (Megagame) draws a lot of players. There could be 1,000 players or just 40; it's the different format that counts. The playing field is often larger than usual, a combination of two or more smaller fields. Usually there are several flag stations. Points are scored for being in control of a flag station at designated times, say 10:00, or by keeping track of eliminations.

Rules

There are many imaginative ways to run a Big Game; there is no fixed format. Twenty-four-hour games are sometimes run, but most are one day. Three or four hours of play may be followed by a lunch break and another three or four hours of play, or it may be six to eight hours straight. Players can walk off the field and take a break anytime in these variations. An eliminated player usually has to check out and sit out for some time before being allowed back in the game.

Tactics

Tactics are hard to plan with Big Games. Stick with your friends as much as you can, and when you can't, make new friends.

These are just a few of many ways to play paintball. Make up your own games if you wish! The two most important things to do are to put safety first and keep the games fun.

Hold That Flag!

Dave Yost

When you play paintball, you're usually playing Capture the Flag, a Boy Scout game in which Team A tries to capture Team B's flag and return the flag to Team A's home base for the victory. You're also playing Tag. You try to tag your opponents out with a paintball shot from your special air gun. Naturally, it's easier to capture the flag when you have tagged your opponents out. Paintball is such a simple game!

Sometimes, though, players want to play variations on the basic game. In fact, the first paintball game had 12 players (each on his own) trying to capture all 12 flags placed on a huge field. Many variations have been suggested over the past decade, different games that create new challenges for all players.

Here is a game I call Hold That Flag! Its foundation is Capture the Flag, but this game also bor-

rows concepts from bridge, poker, and the old television game show "Name That Tune."

The Game in Brief

Hold That Flag is very fast, simple to understand, and easy to score. The action starts instantly and never lets up. It's an intense and focused game. The unique concept of "bidding" for the flag makes the game intriguing. Additionally, the game allows teams to play with or against each other, depending on how the bidding goes.

Summary Three teams are chosen. A single flag is placed nearby in a defendable position. Teams then bid for the flag, that is, they bid to defend the flag. The defending team must hold the flag for as many minutes as they bid. The attack begins. Can the defenders Hold That Flag?

Equipment Needed

1. Flag
2. Stopwatch or timer
3. Scorepad and pencil
4. Whistle or other start- and end-game signal
5. Pair of dice (optional, for game variation)

Pregame All players group together in a central area. The Gamemaster chooses three team captains. They stand, separated, apart from the group. The captains pick teams. As each player is chosen, he or she stands with his or her captain. After three teams are chosen, the Gamemaster auctions off the flag. It goes something like this:

Gamemaster: "*Team 1, what's your bid?*"

Captain 1: "*Team 1 can Hold That Flag for four minutes!*"

Gamemaster: "*Team 2?*"

Captain 2: "*Team 2 can hold it for six minutes!*"

Gamemaster: "*How about Team 3?*"

Captain 3: "*Team 3 can hold it for eight!*"

The captain of Team 1 might call the bid by saying, "Then Hold That Flag!" The captain of Team 2 agrees, saying, "Yeah, let's see you Hold That Flag!" So Team 3 has won the bid for the flag, and it will defend against the combined forces of the other two teams.

Captains bid for the "right" to defend the flag.

The Gamemaster then announces, "Five minutes to go! Teams 1 and 2 withdraw 100 yards." The two attacking teams must now withdraw from the flag area. They must be in one spot, 100 yards away, when the game starts (in five minutes).

Game Begins

When the five-minute prep period expires, the Gamemaster calls "Go!" and the attack begins. The defenders' goal is to keep anyone from the attacking team(s) from touching the flag for the period that they bid, in this case, eight minutes. The two attacking teams must get to that flag before the bid time expires. The attacking teams do not have to stay together as teams. They can mix up and combine their forces in any way they

Two teams will attack; one will defend.

wish. Or they can stay together as two separate teams and attack from opposite sides or from both the front and the rear of the flag station.

Scoring

If the defending team can Hold That Flag for the time bid, they receive two points. If the attackers overcome the resistance before the time is up, each attacking team receives one point.

As soon as the time limit is up or the flag is captured, that round is over. The captains immediately rebid the flag and start another round. A good Gamemaster may get in four rounds an hour, assuming there are not too many players and that

players do not take any long breaks or spend much time getting paint and air. There can be four to eight total rounds per game. An eight-round game should take from two to two-and-a-half hours.

Strategies

With the defending team outnumbered two to one, it's usually inevitable that it will be overrun. The real question is how long a team can defend the flag. Strategy in this game relies heavily on the team captains' abilities to calculate the offensive and defensive strengths of the other teams and the degree of difficulty in defending the flag as it has been positioned for the current game.

The attacking teams can work together.

The strongest team may lose because it bid too high for the flag. It may lose by allowing another team to bid so low that it's not possible to touch the flag before the time limit is up. Generally speaking, the Gamemaster should select the flag position so that five or six minutes is about as long as is probably necessary for the offense to take the flag.

The intriguing part of the game is playing a little poker and bluffing the other captains into bidding way too high for the flag. Then, once they've been wiped out a few times, you try to get the flag for such a ridiculously low bid that they can't possibly touch the flag in the time allowed.

Offensive Tactics

The Gamemaster gives a five-minute warning. At the end of that time, the game actually starts. Be sure that the offensive teams are ready to go immediately. In most cases, the offense *can* take the flag; it's just a matter of time. But do they have *enough* time? Don't take chances; be ready to get into action immediately upon the *Go!* signal from the Gamemaster.

While you are waiting for the signal to go, watch the area you will be attacking. Assign a couple of the sharper players to "intelligence" duty. See if they can determine the areas that will be the most strongly defended, and, if possible, identify the weakest point in the defense.

The amount of time that the flag must be defended will determine the overall attack strategy. When the time is short, go for the flag. If the time is long, go for the defenders. If the defenders made a cheap bid, that is, if they have to defend for only two or three minutes, the attack must be hard and fast. There will not be time to chip away at the defending players from safe cover. Flanking and eliminating individual defenders is time-consuming. The trick with attacking low-time bids is to find the weakest front and go for the flag immediately. However, if the defending team paid dearly for the flag, that is, if they bid too high (eight or more minutes), the attackers have time to work their obvious superior strength into flanking positions to pick off the individual defenders. Once the defenders are thinned out a bit, the flag can be assaulted.

Both teams on offense are striving for the same goal: touching the flag. Use your players effectively. The offensive players can be mixed any way the captains choose. For example, the entire defensive position might be surrounded or two small flanking patrols might chip away at the defense, followed by a major frontal assault. The two offensive teams might each act as separate teams and mount two separate actions; perhaps one comes in from the front and the other from the rear, or they make two assaults on opposing flanks.

One tactic is automatic. If there is less than one minute left in the bid period and the attackers have not been able to touch the flag, then they

Defenders must stall the attack.

must make a full-scale, all-team assault. Everybody goes for the flag!

Not being tagged out when the game ends does not win points, and if you don't touch the flag before the time limit expires, the defenders win. With one minute to go there is no time for clever moves, thrusts, and parries. Have the captain shout a predetermined signal, like "Surfers Rule!" or something to that effect. When the attackers hear that signal, it's "full speed ahead" for every attacker. There is no overtime in Hold That Flag.

Defensive Tactics

The defensive team must never forget its sole mission: Protect the flag for the period of the bid. The only thing that matters is keeping the attackers away from the flag. Keep them at bay. Shoot paint at them to keep them back. You don't have to tag them out except when they're rushing at the flag, so the defense must not get focused on that. Defenders must not leave good cover to chase opponents.

The Gamemaster must set the limits on how far the defenders can be from the flag. Then it's the captain's job to position the defending team so that all routes to the flag are well covered. If one brave player can run through a thinly defended area and get to the flag, the defenders lose the round. Eliminations mean nothing if the flag gets touched; the flag is everything!

Outnumbered two to one, the defenders should avoid direct confrontations since the numbers are against them. Instead, they must make the attackers come to the defenders. Dig in

To win the game, an attacker must touch the flag.

and wait. Make them come into the open in their quest to take the flag.

Never forget there is a time limit. The name of the game for the defenders is *stall!* Hold the attackers back as long as possible. Be quiet and innocuous at the start. Hide to keep the attackers from knowing where all the defenders are. Don't rile up the attackers. Try to keep them relaxed and slow to start the attack. If they are not psyched up, they may waste valuable time getting into action.

Use intelligence officers just as the attackers do. You can assign a couple of players to watch the attackers and try to determine from which direction the attacks will come. Be ready to shift defending players to suit the situation.

Again, the attackers must come to the defenders or lose. As "Old Hickory" might well have said, "Hold your fire until you see their eyes through their goggles!" If attackers want to sit back and shoot at the defenders, the defenders should just hunker down and let them waste their paintballs. The defenders do not ever have to leave their positions. They need only to wait out the time limit. This is their most important tactical advantage.

Variations

Variation One If merely touching the flag proves too easy, the Gamemaster can specify that it must be captured and run out of the defending team's area of control to a predetermined goal or for a predetermined distance. If the flag runner is tagged, he or she must drop it on the spot, but another offensive player may pick it up and carry it on (live-flag rule). Defensive players can likewise pick it up and replace it where the Gamemaster originally placed it.

Variation Two An interesting deviation from the bidding process is to rotate the defense of the flag among the three teams *without bidding*. The team captain defending the flag for that round rolls two dice. The total number on the dice determines how long the team must Hold That Flag. Scoring is as in the regular game. Six rounds (each team defending twice) make a good game.

Variation Three Play six rounds (each team defending twice), and play each round until the flag is touched. The winner is the team able to defend the longest total time for its two times on defense.

Variation Four Play the basic game, but at a specified game time (set by the Gamemaster) the defenders are free to go anywhere the attackers can go. That is, they no longer must stay within the defensive team's boundaries. A defensive team may want to attempt to send one or two players out to flank or "back-door" the attackers, and thus help the defenders protect the flag.

Hold That Flag!

13

How to Play Speedball

Jessica J. Sparks

Speedball! That's "paintball in the arena" in case you didn't know. Speedball is up close and personal, nowhere to run, nowhere to hide, nowhere to pretend you didn't miss that shot.

Paintball started as a game played in the woods. Sneaking and peeking, hiding in natural terrain—these were the skills a good player developed. Then paintball came out of the woods and into the arena, where spectators could watch the game. Today, more and more fields and tournaments are including speedball fields in the mix of game fields. Why? The games go faster, players get more games, those who don't play can watch, those who are tagged out early can watch the rest of the game, and the refs can see when someone is hit a lot easier than in the woods—need more reasons?

The neat thing about arenaball is that you don't need a lot of land to have a field. An area as small as 40 yards by 20 yards can host a game. A better size is 100 yards by 60 yards or so. Another nice thing is that an arenaball tournament doesn't have to be for teams of fifteen, or ten, or seven. It can be one on one, two on two, three on three, and so forth. Five-player is fairly well accepted, but so are smaller team sizes.

Bunkers

In the arena, what a player has for cover might be inflatable, built of construction plastic tubing, or built of plywood. The best fields are the ones where the cover is tall enough so that players can stay on their feet because that encourages action. Low bunkers do nothing but cause players to sit and bore the audience. The best fields are designed so that players are not always seen when they move, adding an element of surprise.

Speedball fields can use wooden bunkers.

Uniforms

Uniforms can be of bright colors that you proba-bly wouldn't wear in the woods. A team might have dark pants and light top or light pants and dark top—or uniforms, like football teams, with player names and numbers on the jerseys. Sponsors might have the sleeves, legs, and what-ever else they can negotiate to advertise them-selves. Camouflage, while acceptable, need not be the uniform of choice.

Uniforms can be colorful for speedball.

Referees

Speedball refs have to have sharp eyes and know the game well, because the games go very quickly in the arena. In the arena an elevated stand for refs might be set up so that one or more of the refs could be above the playing field, which would give them better angles to make some calls.

Television

The nice thing about arenaball is that it can be covered by TV cameras. With one for an over-head-establishing shot and others for sideline and endzone shots as in other sports, paintball becomes even more TV-viewer friendly. For TV viewing it would be good to play arenaball with a

Inflatable bunkers

Speedball!

larger ball that moved more slowly. Hayes Noel, a founder of paintball, suggested that. Whether this comes to the sport remains an open question.

Walk-On Play

When only a few customers show up at a field, say early in the day, it's a good idea to give them games to play. Send them over to the arenaball field to get started. They can rotate onto each team. Never mind the armbands; everyone should be able to keep track of four teammates, and as fast as the first five-on-five is over, the next one begins. Think of this as a warm-up drill that also lets new players get the hang of the game before they go into the woods where it's a little tougher to under-

stand the flow of the play. To keep the games fun, disallow hard-core bunkering.

Speedball also works well as the day winds down. When the number of players dwindles but the playing day is not over, a field can offer speedball as a great way to get in a lot of fast-action games with only a few players. Even if the field has only two players, they can go against one another in the arena, over and over again, learning new skills. A field that does not have an arena can simulate arenaball play in a gully ("gully wars" where you can't retreat or climb out but must move forward to win) or on a flat area ("town wars" where you have to stay in a small area and move forward to win).

When there are more players, running seven-on-seven games works in almost all speedball

Speedball fields may use this heavy-duty "plastic" tubing.

Spectators watch speedball action from behind netting.

fields. Some can hold ten on ten, too. These games can run during the day as a rotation, and give the players a taste of something different from games in the woods. The idea is to run short games so that no one sits out for long, keeping the games going and the paint flying.

Tournaments

Speedball is a tournament promoter's dream. It produces fewer hassles about players who continue to play with a hit on them, fewer hassles about players who overshoot, and so forth, making it a welcome game.

When a promoter wants to include pumpgun or stockgun events, what better place than in the arena? Let those semishooting players play with a pump where everyone can see whether they have been hiding behind a wall of paint or truly are skilled players!

All About Paintchecks

Action Pursuit Games **staff**

The paintcheck is not a simple thing. Basically, either a ref or a player checks another player for a mark or a player checks himself for a mark. But it's not all that simple when you take a deeper look.

Formal Paintchecks

A "formal" paintcheck in today's paintball world is one that shuts down the entire field or a section of the field. It is rarely used. It is mainly for sorting out things after a large firefight or for safety reasons.

Here's how it should work. During the game, a player may call "Paintcheck!" The referee may then blow a whistle one time and yell "Paintcheck!" This means a "formal" paintcheck is happening. All shooting and movement must stop immediately. Everyone is neutral, and author Frank Hughes suggests that gifts and phone numbers may be exchanged. Once the check is complete, only the referee who called it has the power to signal "Game On!"

Ideally, the entire game shuts down for a formal paintcheck. It does not work well to try to limit a formal check to a specific area because imaginary boundaries possess remarkable fluidity. As Hughes, an experienced referee, points out, it is hard to stand powerless while 50 feet away opponents move on your flag. Few people do.

Informal Paintchecks

For the standard "Hey, ref, check that guy!" nearly all paintball fields and tournaments use informal paintchecks. The informal paintcheck involves two people: the referee and the player who was allegedly hit. Hughes calls the informal paintcheck "the second greatest innovation in paintball" (the first being the 20-minute, instead of two-hour, game). Play continues while the referee makes the check. The occasional confusion and inconsistency are a small price to pay for an uninterrupted game (and, Hughes points out, countless opportunities to "accidentally" shoot a referee).

"Hey, ref, he can't shoot me! I called paintcheck!" Bzzzzzz. Sorry. You can call for a paintcheck, but only a referee can initiate one. No player is "neutral" until the whistle is blown (in a formal check) or until the referee reaches him, touches him, and calls him neutral (in an informal check). The universal neutral signal used in tournament play is that the ref, when he is close enough to check the player, holds a white towel high up in the air. The ref should never call someone neutral until he has reached the player. Once opponents see the ref give the paintcheck neutral sign, all shooting and movement toward that player must stop.

The ref has the option to check a player without calling him neutral. The ref may say "Play on" to let the player know he is not neutral. The player can ask "Am I neutral?" or plead "Call me neutral!" but that does not make the player neutral unless and until the ref touches him and gives the paintcheck neutral sign. This means the player needs to take cover until he has been checked. If he plays on and is marked, he is subject to being penalized. That's the player's option. If he takes a hit while being checked and has not been called neutral, he is out. If he has been called neutral and takes a hit, that hit does not count, and the ref may penalize the other team for shooting at a neutral player.

Can nearby players move on you while you're being checked? If a player is not neutral, he or she is still fair game and can be moved on. If you are

neutral, however, no, opposing players may not improve position against you as you're being checked. Nor may they freeze a player to move on the flag. The ref has the option to penalize or reposition the opponents for misuse of the paintcheck rule to gain an unfair advantage. In reality, a player always must keep his or her eyes open and on the opponents while being checked. The point of a check is not to interrupt the game, and sometimes bad things happen to good people.

When to Shoot

Can you shoot a player who has called for a paintcheck on himself? Sure, unless and until the ref reaches and touches him, giving the paintcheck neutral sign. He is not neutral, and too many players will call "paintcheck" to try to get you to stop shooting at them when they are in a bad situation.

Can you shoot a player you have called a paintcheck on? (You sportsman, *you!*) The player is not neutral, and it can be tempting. In a walk-on game, if the player is nicely waiting to be checked, the courteous thing is to stop shooting and let the player be checked. In a tournament, generally all bets are off, and he's fair game until the ref calls him neutral. And one would keep shooting anytime the opponent is continuing to shoot or tries to get away.

After I've been checked, shouldn't I have time to get away if I'm not hit? Well, as Hughes says, there is no guarantee of a "Get Out of Jail Free" card in paintball. In a walk-on game, if the paintcheck has been called, the ref may give a player a three- or a five-count to run; that's the ref's option. This time to get away should not be given to a player who called a paintcheck, since he or she is usually trying to get the other player or players to stop shooting (often a desperation move). In a tournament, rules for a player who has been checked may or may not allow a three- to five-count to run away or take a new position (that is, read the rules).

If you request a paintcheck, doesn't the referee have to do it? No. And especially not if he or she suspects you are using the paintcheck to flush players from hiding. A good referee is not your bird dog, Hughes says. Find the hidden players for yourself.

Are you "dead" (eliminated) if you were hit after the ref reached and touched you and gave the neutral sign? You're not if a ref saw the ball hit you and knew it was a late hit. The idea is to stay in cover until you are checked.

There you have the basics. The more you play, the more paintchecks you will see and call, and the clearer this will all be.

How to Build a Winning Team

Askel Arnesen

A time comes in every paintball player's life when he or she will tire of walk-on games at the field and desire to move into the wide realm of tournaments and team play. If you like a change of pace every once in a while, getting hooked into a team is the best thing for you.

Tournament teams come in all sizes, but the most common sizes are five and ten players, usually with a few alternates. If you're the only person you know who enjoys playing paintball, look for a team that will take you under its wing. There are paintball teams springing up right and left, and if you inquire about teams at your local field, the refs and workers can give you plenty of information.

Finding a Team

The key words to remember when you're looking for a team are *skill*, *location*, *age*, and *level*.

Skill

The team members' skill level, compared to yours, is a very important part of the equation. If you are several times better than any one player on the team, you'll be threatening to the captain and make the other players look bad. On that team, you probably wouldn't enjoy paintball nearly as much compared with playing against people who are about your skill level.

This works both ways. If you realize that you'll be the worst player on the team by far, you have two options. One, if team members still want you, stick with the team and try as hard as you can to learn as much as you can from them and drastically improve your game. Your other choice is to assess that you wouldn't enjoy being the weak link in the chain, and find some other players who are just looking to have some fun.

Location

The team's location is another thing to consider. If the rest of the team lives in Arizona, and you live up in New York, perhaps this team isn't right for you. That's a slight exaggeration of the real problem. Transportation and practices become much more difficult if you live more than a few hours' drive away from the rest of your team. When you live close, you can even ride in car pools.

Age

How important is age? Well, if you're a married man at the ripe age of 40, you might not fit in with a group of 16-year-olds who are out to have a blast. Don't ignore the age difference. It can become a stumbling block for the team's dynamics. Also, if you're 16, I don't think you should look for a team of 30-year-olds to play with because you probably would feel more at home with people the same age as you.

Level

The kind of level refers to the equipment players on the team use. If you notice they all have shiny Shockers with nitrogen systems, your pumpgun may seem slightly out of place. It's a good idea to play with players that have a budget like yours, so you don't get jealous of other players' setups. It's nice to play with someone that has a $1,000 'gun, but you may feel your 'gun is lacking after a while.

Starting a Team

If you play with a few friends regularly and want to get a little more organized, creating a team is the way to go. Creating a team is the simple part. Simply choose a captain and a name. For choosing a captain, look to the player with the most experience and best leadership skills. If you want everyone on your team to be happy about the team name, it's usually good to have the members brainstorm some names and then agree to one.

Finding players for the team can be somewhat more difficult. If you're desperate, spend the day hanging out at your local field and see if anybody's interested in joining. You should be able to create a roster with the names and phone numbers you pick up at the field.

If you're unsure about the skills of your team's members, try several practice games at the field with different members playing the role of captain and see who performs better. Remember, even good captains lose sometimes, so don't base your decision on whether you won, but rather on how the captain reacted to the problems that arose.

Once you have your team members, usually five or ten players, and have selected a captain and team name, you're officially a team. To reinforce that idea, you can take pictures of your team and send them to your local paper, create a team website on the Internet, and inform your local field about the times you're planning on playing there. With some coordination with your field manager, you can play against other teams rather than just five random opponents.

Practice Builds Winning Skills

Practice, practice, practice. Your team doesn't become good by staying home and watching TV. You need to set regular practice times. Depending on how far you want your team to go, these can occur weekly or every other week. Make sure you meet at least once a month, if nothing else. To be a team, you need to feel like a team.

If you're interested in participating in a tournament, practice becomes all the more important. Try to practice for a specific tournament. For example, if the tournament you're interested in playing in is a standard Capture-the-Flag game with a three-minute time limit, practice exactly that kind of game. If possible, use the same facility the tournament will be held in. Practice at least two months in advance for a large tournament.

What should your team practice? Individual games (5-on-5 or 10-on-10) are good practice and fun, but to make a team great and to reach professional status, you'll have to practice skills, which usually are less fun. If you're the captain, it's a good idea to organize a day of practicing skills between games so that you have a chance to try out the skills without anyone getting bored. Common skill builders include:

- shooting while running
- zigzagging to bunkers
- shooting long-distance targets
- working with a teammate to look for a flag
- shooting left- and right-handed from behind trees and bunkers
- sniping
- crawling
- hand and head signals

Another good option for practicing is to have your side playing with only pumps, and have your opponents all use semis. This drill teaches you how to beat the odds, and you have to try your hardest to overcome the semis. It's a great way to grow as a team and learn to depend on one another.

Start a team! It keeps your interest in paintball strong.

Twos and Threes

When you have your team put together, practice scrimmaging against yourselves. Divide up and play two versus three, or five versus five. Make sure you're in a pair or a triad, though, and practice as if you're the only players left on your team. Having someone act as your wing or your point is an advantage, and with team play it becomes a necessity. By breaking into smaller groups, you have a much better chance of surviving and achieving the game's objective.

It's usually good to pair a crawler with a sniper that will cover him, or to place the best and the worst players together so that the better player can compensate for the weaker player. Practice different pairings and see which ones yield the best results.

Once the players on your team have their skills mastered, and they know their 'guns inside out, playing games is the most important thing you can do. After all, to be a team you must practice and play as a team, not as five individual "commandos." Building team relations is important. Usually, the members on your team will naturally become good friends. The thing to avoid is allowing disagreements to inflate into fights.

At practice, teammates help each other improve.

Practice shooting left-handed and right-handed.

Paintball teams are not born overnight or even over a few weeks. Teams take time, and depending on how often you meet together, that time can drag out. If you want a professional team, you have to practice like a professional team, that is, very often. Don't expect your team just to fall into place and the players to pick up the skills they need. Remember, you're dealing not with models but human beings, and people have weaknesses and strengths. If you aren't willing to be patient and give your team as much time as it needs, you might as well not bother starting a team.

Tournaments

Once your team has mastered the essential skills, you're ready to enter some tournaments, so go for it. The more tournaments you're in, the better your team will get and the more fun it will have. Besides playing, there's usually plenty of nifty new gadgets and 'guns to gawk over at tournaments.

And if you're any good, you can walk away with some prizes.

Most players find that the best thing about tournaments isn't whether they win or lose or what kind of prizes they end up with, but seeing other players that are better. If your team has been practicing drills for a while, and an opponent on the team you're playing against wastes you, don't be afraid to talk with him after the game and see if he has any suggestions for how you can improve your game. Seeing players better than you adds to your perspective and gives you something to shoot for. Most experienced players would be honored to give you a few tips or teach you a few tricks. All you have to do is ask.

Remember throughout the tournament not to take it too seriously. If it is your first time, there is a good possibility you won't place very well. But

All teams should scrimmage to improve their skills.

your team needs tournaments to become more united and focused, and when you walk away, you'll know exactly where you need to improve.

Remember, paintball is supposed to be fun! If you're not having fun playing, loosen up some and don't take it so seriously. And if it's still not fun for you, why are you wasting your money and your time?

Equipment

After most teams get started, a major goal is for each player to buy personal, permanent paintball equipment. You can't have a team that's renting equipment every time. Your team members need to get their own 'guns and masks. Your paintball gear is like your car: It is an extension of your personality. It will probably be different for every member of the team because of such factors as budget, style of play, look, and feel. Many players narrow down the field to a few 'guns and then pick the one that looks the coolest.

Some team equipment you might look into would be a bulk CO_2 tank, a scale, and a fill station, so you can refill your own bottles and save a lot of money. Your team members who do fills must be well trained in the proper safety procedures for filling CO_2 before you take this step. The bulk tank can be rented or purchased. It is handy to have extra on-field CO_2 tanks in case you have a problem with the one you're using, use all your

CO_2 and are not close to a commercial field, or are between games at a tournament and need a fresh bottle but don't have time to get a fill or to wait for it to warm up.

Paintballs are another thing to buy together. Buying cases of them allows you a discounted price. A chronograph is a must if you play a lot on your own or scrimmage other groups at private fields—or use an area of a commercial field but must provide your own reffing and safety enforcement.

If you have 10 players on your team or some extra money to throw around, the team's buying one or more "field packages" can be a good idea. With most field packages you get 10 or 20 'guns, masks, loaders, tanks, and more, all ready to go. This is a great cache to have if you're trying to recruit more people into paintball. You can let them try out the setup; then, if they enjoy it and wish to continue playing, you can simply sell them that 'gun package. If your team normally plays with semiautos and you buy a field package

Crawling is an important game skill.

Paintball teams are not born overnight.

of pumpguns, you can have the team switch to simpler 'guns every now and then to try different methods of playing.

If you want to be as stylish as you want to be safe, team jerseys are worth looking into. Besides making your team look sharp and professional, team jerseys will make your team's members feel sharp and professional when they're playing in matching shirts.

Sponsorship

If your team is dynamite and wins some regional or national championships (which is possible), it may be approached by big-name paintball companies wishing to sponsor the players. If no company contacts you, contact some and tell them about your team. Sponsorship offers usually contain discounts on paintball items, occasional free gear, and up-to-date information about what the newest toys in paintball are. It also comes with definite responsibilities. Most sponsored teams have to use their sponsor's product (for example, John Silver Paintballs), and sponsors usually require a team to wear specific jerseys or patches.

But most of us won't be sponsored by the big brand names. So be sponsored locally. Write up a schedule of what your team will be doing in the next six months and hit all the local shops. Maybe someone will sponsor you with burritos, maybe someone with CO_2, maybe a hotel will let you stay a few nights for free. As long as you advertise your sponsor and receive a lot of attention, companies are usually glad to sponsor you.

Remember above all else: Paintball teams are not born overnight. Be patient. Be persistent. Be positive. And if you're having fun, you are a better advertisement for paintball.

Be patient. Be persistent. Be positive.

Spies and Trolls 'R Us
Paintball Scenario Games

Bret Golihew

Paintball scenario games are large-scale recreational games with a story line. Unlike tournament play, scenario game players don't really win or lose. Both the victors and the vanquished have a lot of fun and go home satisfied. The thrill of victory in a scenario game is real, but there is no loss of honor or respect in being on the losing side. Being there and enjoying the camaraderie and friendships of players from distant fields makes all the players winners. Scenario games are among the most rewarding experiences paintball can provide.

Fantasy Fun

The first thing to understand about a scenario game is that it is a fantasy event. It's a fun event. Themes can be futuristic like *Star Wars* or fantasy games like trolls and magicians. Often a theme is tied to a real-life military event, such as a particular battle in World War II or Vietnam, but it might just as well be a takeoff on a movie. The most popular themes are science fiction and action movies, TV shows, and historic or military events.

The theme, as depicted in pregame advertising, is often the main reason players attend scenario games. If you're new to this experience and have some doubts, remember this: When you take a look at the fantasy theme for an upcoming event, don't take the theme seriously. Think of it, for example, as staging a reenactment of the Japanese attack on Pearl Harbor using squirt guns and water balloons. Everybody gets wet, nobody gets hurt, and you might even learn something.

Paintball is paintball, no matter what the theme. If you follow the safety rules and wear proper safety equipment, the only fear that should

Scenario game players may dress for the role.

be felt in a scenario game is not having enough money to buy more paint.

The critics of history-based scenario games attack paintball scenario games as they do any historical reenactments by people shooting firearms that use only blanks. They criticize the battles for areas of the world held by Society for Creative Anachronism—modern-day knights of the Middle Ages who fight with light weapons, heavy weapons, and body armor. What these critics don't understand is that the theme is a creative tool the writer of the scenario game uses to set up certain situations. It allows particular characters, locations, and movements to be applied to the groups of players. The game, as played out, can be applied to almost any place and time— past, present, or future. The theme can, however, allow prospective players a mental head start on the game.

Game Types

Most scenario games are played on large fields, meaning players operate in a 360-degree envi-

ronment, not in the "forward only" focus of tournaments. The scenario game teaches players about energy, about paint conservation, how to lead and how to follow, effective communication methods, the honor of how you play instead of how you win, and, finally, how to meet people and have a great time without the pressure syndrome of high-performance failure.

The different types of paintball scenario games have a few things in common, and knowing these can help you create a successful event. Planning and preparation are the key factors of a good scenario game. Writers start with a theme for the game and an accurate map of the playing field. These are used to set the boundaries of who can do what and where they can do it.

A common feature of scenario games are "hospital" and "medic" rules. These special scenario game features enhance the players' game experience by providing a method to return them to the game after their elimination, since the game doesn't stop every 20 minutes like a regular paintball game. Scenario games can be placed into two main categories: single-day games and 24-hour games.

Single-Day Games

The most common type is the single-day scenario game. Good for both large and small fields, it is relatively easy to set up and run. The single-day's advantage over the 24-hour is the shorter time investment for the field and the players. Such a game is usually 8 to 12 hours long and normally played in daylight only. Single-day scenario games can be divided into two main variants: mission orientations and the Big Game.

Fantasy vehicles are part of scenario games.

Mission Orientation

The best type of game for small fields, mission-oriented scenario games divide the day into a series of time periods for various missions. The total group of players present is divided into two equal groups, and a leader for each is selected. Each mission begins in the break or assembly area with the two team leaders being given a map and written mission orders for the next game.

The teams must perform opposing mission assignments within a specified time. When that time expires, or when the mission of one team is accomplished, the players return to the break area and receive the next mission. The game can be played with the teams alternating offense and defense roles, with the defending team entering the field first.

The advantage in this type of format is that it offers the producers excellent control of the overall scenario game through the use of (1) written mission orders for each game, (2) selected areas designated and prepared in advance, and (3) set times for each mission and for breaks. A typical single-day, mission-oriented scenario game allows up to 12 30- to 45-minute missions with 15-minute breaks between the missions.

Props Mission-oriented scenario games rely heavily on the use of props—objects placed on the field before the game. The field is usually "seeded" with such props as ammo boxes, document envelopes, a dummy, or unusual items (for example, a balloon tied to a tree or a cooler full of soda). Placing these objects on the field in advance reduces the task of running the props out to their correct position before each mission.

During the course of a mission, the offense team has the task of locating an object and returning that object to the break area, while the defense team must act to prevent that from happening. Other missions might be setting up ambushes, attempting to capture or eliminate a specific enemy player, or the classic rescuing of a downed pilot.

The Big Game

The popular single-day Big Game format is great for large fields. It is best characterized by its simplicity. Often arranged as an annual event, some Big Games are run as benefits for local charities. Usually the scenario aspect of the game is not as detailed as for a 24-hour scenario game or as structured as for a mission-oriented game. A Big Game normally runs six to eight hours and ends with a climactic battle.

The Big Game starts with each side being given control of half the field, with each half containing several strategic areas that must be defended from capture. Usually, these areas will include the headquarters, an ammo dump, a village, or a fort. The object of the game is to control those sites for a certain length of time to score points.

Props, such as dummy missiles, ammo boxes, or drums, are used to provide movable objectives for special mission recovery. Sound effects and

special "surprise" staged events are used to spice up the action, and, where safe, controlled pyrotechnics may be used as well.

Third Forces Often this type of scenario game employs a small third force on the field to act with independent goals or to be available as an ally team. Occasionally these players have "special powers" and reduced vulnerability to ordinary paintballs; they can be eliminated only through unconventional means, such as a paint grenade or a smoke grenade.

Vehicles Vehicles are also popular with the Big Game scenario game. Everything from trucks, helicopters, hovercraft, and "paintball tanks" have made appearances at them. Paintball tanks are becoming routine at scenario games.

24-Hour Games

Twenty-four-hour scenario games are the most complex and involved type of game for both the players and the fields. They were practically invented by, and have been greatly popularized by, the master of the genre, Wayne Dollack. He and his wife, Jackie, travel to paintball fields in their motor home, spreading their unique brand of paintball mind game to an eager and enthusiastic audience. They operate Wayne's World, near Ocala, Florida (www.waynes-world.com). The key to Dollack's success with the 24-hour format is that, like a traveling road show, Dollack brings a highly organized and professional system to fields that otherwise would never have attempted to produce scenario games of such complexity. The Dollacks' effective advertising and skillful game

Special props can be part of scenario games.

designs have set a standard for 24-hour games that few producers can match.

Participating in a Dollack scenario game is a unique experience. Missions go out to both teams by radio. Each player gets a detailed identity to role-play. Audio and pyrotechnic effects are used to create an appropriate atmosphere. Role-playing spies play their parts on the field and in the break area. You can play the game on many different levels: as hunter, soldier, or spy. For 24 hours, you are in Wayne's World.

Basic 24-Hour Game

The basic 24-hour Dollack game has fixed elements. Each team controls a headquarters area. Wayne calls in missions to each side by radio every 15 to 30 minutes. The team generals send out squads with mission order cards to complete those missions. If the mission is completed, a ref signs off on the card and turns it in for points.

At the same time, other role players are at work in secret meetings, sabotaging missions, selling and trading information and game props, and in general trying to cause the enemy as much confusion and trouble as possible. You just won't know whom you can trust.

Day and Night

The 24-hour scenario game divides the day into three sets. Set 1 is a day game (from noon on Saturday to dusk on Saturday), followed by an hour stand-down (to set up for the night game). Set 2 is a night game (from after the stand-down until dawn on Sunday morning) with another stand-down for breakfast. Set 3 is a Sunday morning game that ends at noon on Sunday.

After the game ends, everyone meets for an assembly. It includes an announcement of the winner, a few short speeches and thanks to the sponsors, and many prizes and awards for participants.

Players

Scenario games offer a role to everyone in the game. Some are very complicated, most are simple and easy to do, but all are about the most fun you can have while playing paintball! Here are the basic characters or roles to play:

• **The General.** No matter what type of scenario game you play in, there will be some sort of command structure. If you are lucky enough to be named a General or a Commanding Officer

(CO), use your command wisely. Always remember that the individual player is a paying customer of the field and must not be abused by your authority as leader. Never ask a player to perform any task that you would be unwilling to do. You have a great responsibility to lead the other players on your team by good example. If you are abusive, your subordinate teammates will either act like you or may defect to the enemy and frag you. This really does happen.

• **Undercover Agents.** Enemy players are specifically tasked with hunting you down. Watch out! Some of them can be very devious. An enemy type to beware of is the spy or traitor. It is almost certain that some of your own players will actually be undercover agents working for the enemy, patiently waiting for the best moment to strike.

If role-playing is involved, be careful whom you trust. Don't accept any envelopes or packages; they may be booby-trapped. Make no mistake about it, in a scenario game eliminating a general or his command staff can score big points.

• **The Executive Officer (XO).** This person is the team's second-in-command. The duties of the XO are to assist the General with the running of the team and in the absence of the General to take full command of the team.

• **Platoon and Squad Leaders.** These players execute the mission orders from the command staff. When a mission is accomplished, they are responsible for providing the necessary proof of completion to the headquarters (HQ).

- **Role Players.** In a Dollack game, there are players who show up just for the role-playing. The role players have their own game going inside the larger scenario game. They have a major impact on the overall outcome of the game. An important point to remember about most scenario games is that missions win games, but role players can outscore mission points. If you accept a role to play, you are provided with specific goals to accomplish in the game. It is very important that you try to maintain your character's integrity and motives as they were given to you. The game director will provide you with certain props and meeting times. Preserve the continuity of the game by staying in character and not taking over the game with your own private agenda.

- **Grunts.** Most players in a scenario game are grunts. As a grunt, your obligation is to perform the tasks or missions that the team leaders give out. This is not to say that all orders must be blindly followed. The important part is to complete the mission in the time allowed. If you have a good understanding of what is required, you won't need much direction to complete it. Grunts should try to help the team leaders maintain unit cohesion by trying to stay together and operate as a team. Grunts also get important tactical roles. These roles, for example, can be as medics, weapons specialists, combat engineers, or demolition experts. If you play one of these roles, it is important to learn what you can do with the role and use your skill as best you can. Your team depends on your abilities.

Communications

Radio communications can be a major tool in large-scale scenario games. A Dollack game uses them to send missions to the two teams. Each team also uses them for communications between the command staff and individual squads. These are called *radio nets*.

The scenario game director may use three radio nets: one each to the two team command staffs and another to the referees. The two teams each operate several radio nets for squad-to-squad radio communications and for relays among the members of the command staff.

Team Communications

A single radio-equipped team can create a very effective method of control over an entire side. Such a team can take control of a side when one of its members plays the role of General. The General then assigns each of his radio-equipped teammates to positions in each platoon or squad. The General now has people he trusts in each of the squads and can communicate using codes and call signs. This creates an effective command and control structure.

The most common types of radios being used in large-scale scenario games today are FM, UHF sport-type radios and 40-channel CBs. Also short-range FM Vox headset types are useful for squad communications.

One thing to keep in mind whenever you are using a radio to communicate is that it is not secure. Everything you say over a radio net is subject to interception and even jamming by your opponents. Use codes!

The Future

Each scenario game is a unique event. It reflects the character of the field, the practicality of the scenario, and the composition of the players who show up for the game. Scenario games are not for all paintball players, but if you give them even one try, you may find a lot to learn.

As scenario games continue to attract more and more players and to draw teams dedicated to playing them, more fields will recognize the publicity, entertainment, and customer-satisfaction values of the scenario game. Look for a scenario game at a field near you, or ask about the possibility of your favorite field hosting a role-playing event.

Twenty Steps to a Better Game

Jim "Roadrunner" Fox

You are a better player when you learn the skills of the better players. These skills may look like a lot to learn if you try to acquire them all at once, so don't do it that way. Learn and study them one by one. They will become part of your paintball thinking and nature, making you a better player.

1. Plan. Before every game, always formulate some type of plan. Don't just go out and form a skirmish line. Do not let your opponents dictate what moves you need to counter with. Go into a game with offensive moves in mind; if you don't, you will be forced into playing defense.

2. Be different. Do not keep doing the same thing over and over again, whether it's a particular move or it's going to the same places on the field. An experienced player or team will know

Have an offensive game plan.

what you are going to do in a future game. They will devise a strategy to counteract your play.

3. Check your hits. See where you are taking hits on your body and equipment. Work

Exploit the weakest part of your opponents' play.

on moving your body differently to protect those areas. If it's your shoulder that keeps getting hit, probably you're letting it stick out too much from your cover. If it's your goggles, you know what you're doing wrong. For your loaders, take out the ones that take a lot of hits; it's only going to be one or two. You may get hit again in that area, but now your odds of getting a bouncer are higher.

4. Don't tunnel. Scan the field from side to side, and check behind you. Do not get tunnel vision so that you fixate on any particular part of the field.

5. Go where they aren't. Always go where your opponents are not likely to be. Encounter the least amount of opposition possible. Exploit the weakest part of a team or field. This is where your main push should be made.

6. Locate by the clock. To locate an opponent, use the clock method. You say "He's at your 12" to mean "He's right in front of you." To com-

municate that the opponent is on your right, say "He's at my 3." Then shoot to mark the bad guy's cover.

7. Double your odds. Control a key position with two players to double the odds in your favor. If one player gets eliminated, your team will still control the key position. The two players should go for the key position at the same time to force your opponents to concentrate on two players instead of just one—which may distract your opponents and give you an advantage somewhere else, too.

8. Communicate. This is said time and again, but so often it never happens. Use code words and hand signals. All good teams communicate well. Have your floater and spotter communicate clearly and often.

9. Set up to shoot. Get set up in your shooting position before you come from behind your protection to shoot. This saves you valuable time, and you can get the jump on your opponent

Communicate!

Anticipate!

paintgun up to shoot, locate your target, and shoot, you've been out in the open way too long, and probably you'll be eliminated.

10. React fast. React to situations quickly. Even better, anticipate them if you can. Experience is probably your best teacher. Remember with your own moves not to give your opponents time to react, as they will use it to their advantage.

11. Backdoor. Try to backdoor as much as possible. Punch through your opponents' skirmish line and then backshoot several players to open a hole, which then should be pushed by your teammates.

just that much quicker. If you have your paintgun down at your side, pop out and then bring your

Set up before you come up or out to shoot.

Crawl when you need to.

12. Sweet spots. Call out the sweet spots (your opponents' cover). You can pick them out before a game by walking the field, or you can describe and pinpoint sweet spots during play.

13. Retreat low. If you are taking a lot of fire from one or several positions and need to retreat, don't stand up and run away—because you will just get shot in the back. Get on your stomach and crawl out. Do the same thing when you are moving through the field and someone fires on you: Don't run, but instead fall straight down and crawl to your protection.

14. Line of fire. Never have two players directly in line with each other. The paint coming in on the player up front can miss him or her and hit the teammate who is directly in line behind the first player.

15. Marking spots. Use something as a reference point so you can remember where your opponents are. You can remember where they are

by marking their protection with a fresh paint splat or by using an old paint mark or something like a big knot on a log. Line up your opponent with your mark. If you can't find him right away, or you need to shoot at someone else for a bit, you can refer back to your mark.

16. Concentrate paint. Concentrate your paintball firepower. Get two or three paintguns firing on one position. There will probably be no place for that player to go—except out (or maybe he will be able to retreat). If this player tries to slug it out with your players, the odds are against him, and you should take him out.

17. Floaters. Remember to use floaters on your team. These designated players should be able to see the entire playing field. They communicate with the rest of the team. They keep count of how many eliminations both teams have. They can fill in a hole in your team's skirmish line if needed for whatever reason. They can see when to push offensively or pull back defensively.

18. Create diversions. Confuse your opponents whenever possible. For example, start the game with an overload to one side, and then slowly shift over a few players to the other flank. Disguise your initial moves as much as possible.

19. Keep on the move. A moving player is harder to hit and harder to flank than a stationary player. If you are in a good spot, you can move away from it because you can go back to it—and your move will help confuse your opponents. By moving, you keep from being a target at a sweet spot and you take away your opponents' chance of concentrating fire on you.

20. Speed counts. Do not waste time, act timid, or do certain moves too slowly. Being slow on your part will give the opposition time to counteract your moves.

I recommend that you practice these tactics whenever you can. They will help you stay in a game longer, and help you and your team be better paintball players.

Hopperball

Action Pursuit Games **staff**

Hopperball: a paintball game in which participants enter the playing field with no more than one hopper (loader) of paint that holds no more than 200 paintballs.

Hopperball is happening at fields and tournaments. It's a "limited-paint" game for fields to offer groups with low budgets. Hopperball teaches players to focus on accuracy rather than sheer firepower. Adding Hopperball to the long list of ways to play paintball is a way to keep advanced players challenged while also adding to newer players' enjoyment.

The respected PanAm Circuit—that is, the expanded Great Western Series (GWS)—has a limited-paint rule for its tournaments. It's "bring your own paint" (BYOP) or buy it at the event, but for the five-player games, each player gets only 200 balls (one hopperful) for the game. The limited paint gives teams a budget. They know how much

Hopperball is 200 balls per game! These are paintballs at a factory.

paint they will need for the preliminary games, and they can predict what they will need extra for making the playoffs. Teams can either buy locally and bring what they expect to use, or buy at the event (www.panamcircuit.com).

Limited-paint games help keep costs down.

Accuracy is critical in Hopperball.

Hopperball adds a tactical twist to the games. A player used to carrying 1,000 balls will see that he has to change his tactics from "constant dumping" to something else. A player who doesn't change his ways will hear the devastating sound of the last few balls rattling in his hopper, and he'll be looking on the ground or begging for paint from a teammate.

Limited-paint games at the national level also include the one-loader (100 balls-per-game) limit used at the 1999 U.S. Top Gun Indoor National Championships, hosted by Splat-1 Adventures. For these one-on-one arenaball games, the entry fee includes all paint and air, furnished by the event producer. Stockgun games can be run where each player gets two or three tubes a game (a tube holds 10 paintballs).

Games in the Punta Gorda, Florida, area are played with the paint issued before each game. For the first game each player gets 40 paintballs. For each other game throughout the day a player gets an additional 20 rounds. This, according to Allan Reeves, "lets the new players walk on a lot easier. They don't have to worry about getting peppered the first time out. It doesn't cost a fortune. . . . And, finally, for the experienced player, it takes a sure shot and, we think, more skill to actually hit the person right away. None of this spraying the bunker with paint all day. When you're down to three balls left and you're within sight of the flag and [have] no idea of what kind of base defense you're up against . . . that takes skill."

Limited paint reduces spray-and-pray tactics and encourages movement.

Recreational Hopperball games work well for pumpgun and semiauto games, where several brands of hoppers all hold 200 balls, more or less. Experienced field operators offer different kinds of games for their customers, and those who have offered Hopperball have found customers appreciate the game. They say that only a tiny number of players always want Hopperball or limited-paint games. They say that their players want variety to keep paintball interesting—unlimited-paint games, pumpgun and stockgun games, Hopperball, Big Games, tournaments, scenario games, Megagames, Hawaiian shirt days, and so forth.

Players throughout the country are saying they want to see limited-paint games offered. One reason is fun. Another is cost. Still another reason is to even the playing field against the super-high-tech paintgun shooters with unlimited paint. Here's a sample of their opinions.

"I have a friend who has an Angel and it is almost no fun to play against him. As long as he has paint, I am on my belly. If we limit the amount of paint a person can carry, they will have to be more careful as to where they put it. He would still have the advantage he paid for with his marker, but it doesn't overmatch the game so that you must *have a semiautomatic marker. Besides, didn't we learn yet how much an arms race costs? I thought paintballers were smarter than the government."*

Ralph Beatty
Seattle, Washington

"It is a whole different game when people just 'lay on the trigger' and hammer paint at your bunker. It takes the fun out of the game."

Preston McDonald
Memphis, Tennessee

Five balls left?

"I understand that paintball fields are businesses that require revenue to operate. Encouraging 'one-case, one-kill' (shooting a ton of paint to get one player out) helps keep the field open, but the amount of paint being shot is too much! When there is so much paint flying, all the strategy, true skill, and fun are taken out of the game, which is now a game of lobbing balls at players all the way across the field.

"When there is a set ball limit you have to conserve your shots. With conserving shots comes strategy and true skill because you have to ambush the other team, sneak up on opponents, and make your shots count. A group of friends and I have a field of our own that we play on. We make 25-ball limits for the game, and we have fun. Before we start a game, our team will develop our tactics to get behind, isolate, or angle out our opponents.

"I think that field operators should consider placing a few games with set ball limits on their schedules, which would not only cause players to become more skillful but would make that entry-level 'gun competitive with that 'all powerful' Angel Eclipse, and encourage more newbies to play."

Paintballman 2000
Pittsburgh, Pennsylvania

"Limit the amount of paint per player! I don't care if you can shoot 15 paintballs a second if you can only shoot it for 20 seconds! Three hundred to 500 rounds should be enough to win. Persons are less likely to send off strings of 12 paintballs if they know they have only a limited amount of paint to waste."

Chad Wagner
Terre Haute, Indiana

Improve Your Game

Dale Bright

What is fire discipline?

"Being able to consistently hit what you are shooting at. Also, I don't like the spray-and-pray practice that most folks with semiautos use . . . one round per second on target will keep a person pinned down just as well as five rounds per second or more."

Trapper Davis, Splatzone Paintball
Hopewell, Virginia

"Being in complete control of your marker while paying 110 percent attention to what is going on around you."

Todd Peverill, General Manager
Pev's Paintball Pro Shops, Virginia

Overall, most paintball players have pretty much the same idea of what good fire discipline is. For those who don't have much idea, it may be easier to understand the need for good fire discipline by looking at it from a different perspective.

If you played a day of walk-on rec ball shooting 1,000 paintballs in eight games and getting 10 eliminations for the day, you shot 100 balls per elimination. At an average cost of 4 cents per ball, you spent $4 to get each elimination. Suppose that with the use of accurately aimed fire and proper tactics, you got the same 10 eliminations but shot only 500 paintballs. You would have saved a lot of money and you could play more often on the same budget.

If you can play twice as often on the same amount of money, are you going to have more fun? Yes, unless your idea of having fun on the paintball field is to shoot as much paint as you can afford as fast as you can pull the trigger. Education, practice, and playing time are the three keys to improving your game because they improve your fire discipline. Next are ways to improve while having fun at the same time.

The Right Way: Education

All of us who play regularly have an obligation to help less-experienced and younger players understand the techniques and tactics they need to excel in our sport. This is where education comes into the picture. We can do a lot for the future of the sport if we take the time to help newbies understand how the game should be played, instead of using them for target practice and "lighting them up" when they make a mistake on the field.

The new players are the future of our sport, and we must take the time to get them headed in the right direction. A few minutes spent coaching the new players before the start of the game not only helps your team but makes your recreational-paintball day more enjoyable. Remember, rec ball is supposed to be fun.

Education does not stop with the new players. An old quote goes something like "Sometimes a teacher, always a student." In other words, we should never have the attitude that we know it all. We should constantly strive to improve our game. We can all learn a great deal about paintball by simply being observant and keeping an open mind.

Try going to your favorite field sometime and don't play. Just put on your safety gear and go watch a few games. You will be surprised at how much you *thought* you knew about playing that field. An even better way to learn what to do and what not to do is to become a judge or referee. If you ref long enough, you will see it all.

You can also learn from reading *APG, Paintball,* and other magazines dedicated to the game, and the Internet is chock-full of paintball sites where

Controlling your rate of fire is a winning tactic.

you can find most anything you want to know. As with any public forum, the Internet has some good information and some not-so-good information. With time and common sense, you will be able to sort out what is useful to you.

Practice

Reading can help your game, but paintball is a physical activity, and nothing can take the place of playing time and practice. "Practice?" you ask, "Why should I practice when I only play rec ball?" Because paintball is supposed to be fun, and you have more fun when you develop good playing skills.

This doesn't mean that you should run drills all day like the pro-tournament players, but you should devote at least some time to practice at the target range. I recommend at least a few minutes of quality practice at the target range each time

Seek accuracy and practice fire control.

Practice shooting skills.

you go to the field. That small investment of time shooting at targets will greatly enhance your shooting skills and make your game more enjoyable. Jim Jadryev, owner of Check-It Paintball in Chantilly, Virginia, says that fire discipline is "controlling your use and rate of fire." He suggests that the best way to improve your shooting ability is to learn to judge distances and to shoot accurately by practicing at the target range, and to use the best-breaking paint that is consistent with your 'gun.

Spend time at the range developing your shooting skills and learning how your 'gun shoots under different weather conditions and with different paint and barrel combinations. At the target range you can learn the effective range of your 'gun. You can learn to control your trigger finger so that when you shoot, only your finger moves and your 'gun stays on target.

If you have sights on your 'gun, you can make any adjustments necessary at the range. If you don't use sights, you can learn how to sight down the side of the barrel. Make sure you use your

time at the target range wisely. Paintballs are expensive, and we really enjoy shooting them more during a game than at a target on the range, so concentrate on your practice and make sure each paintball you shoot is a learning experience.

Playing Time

Playing time is the best way to improve your game. However, you can learn more from a dedicated effort at trying different tactics and skills than from a game of random attempts to eliminate as many opponents as possible. There are many ways to challenge yourself on the field while learning new techniques and getting in some good practice. The next time you play a walk-on day, pick one or two games during that time to work on some specific skills. If you are playing a semi-auto game, try playing a game of Hopperball.

Hopperball

Hopperball is simply playing with only the paint in your loader. Leave your eight-pod harness at the staging area. Hopperball is a great way to improve your shooting skills and fire discipline because if you don't control the rate of fire, you will be out of paint before you know it.

Accuracy

Another way to help improve shooting skills while playing rec ball is to play with a pump in a game for semiautos (or, better yet, play with a stockgun). This limits even more the amount of paint you shoot, and you really have to concentrate on tactics and aimed fire. Actually, this is quite an easy thing to do if you think about what you are doing and remember to work within your self-imposed limitations.

Some of the semi players may laugh at you when you show up with your Phantom stockgun or start playing with your Angel and only 200 paintballs for the entire game. But they won't be laughing so hard after they have been eliminated by someone who was concentrating on tactics and aimed fire instead of "accuracy by volume."

Play Hopperball to improve your fire discipline.

Aim!

20

How to Get More Paintball Pleasure

Russell Maynard

For most of the people who play the game, a little paintball goes a long way. Paintball is something they do occasionally, maybe two or three times a year. And typically they play on a special occasion, such as a birthday or bachelor party, or as an alternative to boring, annual company picnics. Field owners affectionately call the Occasional Paintball Player "OP" (rhymes with soapy). All of us should love and care for OPs. It's the money they spend on rental equipment and 100-round bags of paint that keeps our fields open.

We should love them, but it is difficult for players like you and me to understand them. How can an OP stand to play only once or twice a year? But then, you and I are addicts. The first time we tried paintball, we got hooked! Like some powerful mind-altering drug, paintball electrified the pleasure center of our brains. We couldn't get enough. The more or better paintball we played, the more or better the fun we had.

This is a cycle well known to field owners. They have seen the transformation of OPs into "WORPs" (walk-on or regular players) thousands of times. From a group of 20 or 30 OPs, maybe two or three players become obsessed. You can see it in their eyes: They love the action, the competition, the paintguns and gear, all of it! And all they can think about is more-better paintball (the more, the better). They *have* to come back the next week . . . and the next week . . . and the next week.

Usually the obsessed buy gear before the end of the first month. Owning instead of renting means they can play more and play better, and the purchase is a rite of passage confirming their growth from OP into WORP. By the end of the second or third month they're talking about how many weekends it's been since they missed a day of play. By the fourth or fifth month they're begging the field owner to let the six of them (they've made friends with some other WORPs by then) play as a team against a private group of 20 or 30 OPs. "Come on. Please. The OPs will have a great time (as we pummel them), honest."

If the new WORPs are friendly and don't develop into the type of players who believe arguing and complaining are important paintball skills, a smart field owner will encourage them to stick around. He'll show the WORPs how to improve as players, maybe let them become involved with the field operation as refs, and help them find ways to feed their need for more-better paintball.

Field owners take care of WORPs as best they can because they know there is a downside to the paintball cycle. For all their initial excitement and enthusiasm, all their declarations of how paintball is the greatest, the ultimate game, the average lifetime of a WORP is only about a year. WORPs typically blame economics as the reason they burn out, but usually that is just an excuse. The real problem is that WORPs hit a point where *more* paintball no longer is satisfying. They need *better* paintball to keep getting pleasure from the game.

Some WORPs cannot make the transition to better paintball. They are the players who quickly reach a plateau and stop improving. These WORPs have good paintguns and can shoot them really fast, but they keep making the same mistakes and missing the same opportunities during games—day after day, weekend after weekend. When a field owner or another player tries to give them advice, the point goes right over their heads or they argue instead of listening. Because they shoot plenty of OPs and pull a flag or two during the day, these WORPs think their abilities are just fine.

There isn't much a field owner can do for this type of WORP. It's a fact of life that once a player stops learning and improving, paintball quickly loses its challenge and ceases to be fun. Soon the OPs this player on a plateau pounds this month will be outplaying him—and he won't understand why. Chances are he'll degenerate into a complainer or a yeller, accusing and blaming everybody and everything except himself. He may try switching to another field with different OPs, but he is just resisting the inevitable. This WORP is on his way out.

Field owners should concentrate their efforts on the other type of WORP instead, the one who wants to learn to play better paintball. When the time comes for these WORPs to move beyond the level of walk-on play (before they begin to stagnate from a lack of competition), a smart field owner helps and encourages them to make the next move, to take the next step. That next step is *tournament play*.

Playing in tournaments is a concept most WORPs resist at first. Their initial response is rejection or denial, and their rationales run the gamut from "tournaments turn players into cheaters" to "we can't compete unless we have sponsors." All these objections are nothing more than covers to hide the WORPs' anxieties. The WORPs may be afraid of losing, unsure of their playing abilities, or just emotionally uncomfortable with the thought of leaving the security of their safe little WORP nest. Usually it's a combination of all three.

The job of the field owner is to help WORPs get past this stage of negativity. He has to encourage them to become "TPs" (tournament players). The first step is reminding players how much fun they had making the transition from OPs into WORPs; the next step, developing from WORP to TP, will be just as exciting and enjoyable.

Playing in tournaments means a person joins or forms a team and learns the teamwork of advanced tactics and strategies. It means making new friends, trying new fields, and experiencing the challenge of higher competition. In short, growing from a WORP into a TP means many more years of more and better paintball for you.

Once the field owner has WORPs thinking positively about tournament paintball, he needs to tell them what it means to become a TP. First and foremost, it means a person must learn to treat paintball as a sport instead of a game. It isn't that TPs are supposed to take paintball so seriously they stop having fun; it's that they need to be sincere and committed in their efforts and realize it will take years of dedication for them to master the sport. TPs should want to work to improve their abilities every time they go to the field.

Becoming a TP also means cultivating the mind-set of a student of the sport. A good TP learns from mistakes, keeps his mind open to new ideas, and is willing to look objectively at his or her strengths and weaknesses as well as those of other paintballers. As long as TPs hold on to these positive attitudes, they continue to grow as players and get more pleasure and satisfaction from paintball.

The first change a field owner should make with a group of potential TPs is to stop them from playing walk-on style paintball. Playing against low-level competition does not take much concentration. When players are not concentrating, their moves become lazy and sloppy, which reinforces bad habits instead of eliminating them. It is better for TPs to play by themselves. Intensive, two- or three-hour sessions of working on individual skills and squad tactics are much more productive than thoughtlessly bashing OPs all day (and they save on paint, too). You need only four or five players to run drills, which should be the main form of practicing for TPs in their early stage of development. If you have enough TPs to run five-on-five scrimmages or practice games, playing a few of these is a good way to end a session.

A smart field owner helps set up and organize these TP practices and invites WORPs with potential to participate. The players who regularly attend these workouts or tryouts won't have the usual problems of forming themselves into teams when it's time to go to a tournament. And as an added benefit, these TP practices can provide a general pool of replacement TPs once teams are established. The transition from OP to WORP to TP is a natural progression for players addicted to more-better paintball. Although these are big steps, they don't have to be difficult steps if a field owner uses his knowledge and experience to help players through them.

One of the first decisions for a team of new TPs is choosing which tournaments to enter and at what level. In general, there are three categories of tournaments (local, regional, and national) and four levels of play (rookie, novice, amateur, and professional). The team of new TPs may play novice or amateur, depending on the rules of various tournaments; neither is professional level. Each team has to answer the question "Which tournaments are right for us?"

Local tourneys typically are one-day events that draw teams only from the immediate area. Usually they attract 10 to 30 teams, five-player sized or smaller. Seldom does a local event separate teams into more than one division. The low number of teams necessitates mixing rookies, novices, and amateurs. Entry fees range up to $350 or so. Sometimes players will be restricted to shooting the event's paint only. Most fields stage at least one local tournament per year. Thus, the number of local events in an area normally depends on the number of fields.

Local tourneys are the most convenient and the most economical (no travel expenses). They also present an opportunity for new teams of TPs to play against other area TPs, which helps all teams develop their competitive skills. And because the amount of prizes and the level of competition generally are lower at local events, the stress of winning or losing also is low. Relaxed players have more fun.

On the other hand, local tourneys have some disadvantages: They can be disorganized or poorly reffed, have weak field layouts, and use confusing or eccentric rules. Local events also can be breeding grounds for petty jealousies, rivalries, and rumors. And if the local team base includes many experienced teams and the event doesn't offer separate divisions, new TPs may get hammered to the point of souring on tournament play.

In summary, WORPs who want to become TPs definitely should get on a team and play local events. It's the cheapest and easiest way to get tournament experience. Just don't expect to win thousands of dollars in prizes. And if things don't go well, don't be thickheaded and judge the quality of all tournaments based on a single local event.

At the other end of the spectrum are the big national tournaments, such as the National Professional Paintball League (NPPL) events, the Zap Amateur, the PanAm majors, and the WPF majors. These usually are three- to five-day events that draw teams from across the continent and sometimes from outside North America. Expect to see 60 to 100 teams attending. Usually there will be multiple events on the schedule, such as

Top Gun, Stockgun, Young Guns, 5-man, or 10-man. These national tournaments draw top-rated teams that want to play against, or be known as, the best teams in the world. Entry fees for 5-player teams run upward of $500 and can exceed $2,000 for 10-player teams.

The advantages of big national tourneys are their offering the highest level of competition and chances to see and experience state-of-the-art paintball play. The newest and most high-tech paintball gear is on display, too. At the Zap Amateur in Pittsburgh, the GWS in Hawaii, and NPPL's World Cup in Florida in 1999, for example, nearly all the leading companies in the paintball industry attended and had a vendor's booth. National events have a track record of success. They award the most prizes to the winning teams, and the teams who win these events are the most likely to attract major sponsorship.

Big national tournaments, however, are the most expensive. Add up your entry fees, travel costs, and paintball budget, and you may find you need more than $1,000 per player to cover expenses. Because so many teams attend, the amount of play you get might be limited; at some big events, a team might only play six games in two days if they don't make the playoffs. And with so much in prizes or money at stake (and the potential of getting or losing sponsorship), the frustration level at nationals often runs extremely high. Do not expect your competition to be friendly and helpful, and things get even tenser during playoffs. Tempers flare. No matter how hard tournament promoters try to keep the mood friendly and fun, the intensity of competition at big national events can take a toll on sportsmanship.

In summary, big national tournaments are paintball happenings that every TP must experience eventually. The question is, how do you know when you are ready for them? The best advice is to play local and regional events first to gain experience before tackling the big time. And don't blow your team's entire annual tournament budget on just one big event.

The mid-range in tournament play is regional events. Usually these events are part of an annual circuit series, with each stop on the series designed to draw teams from a region of the United States. Examples of regional tourneys include the PanAm Circuit, the WPF/Zap series, the Mid-South Paintball Association (MSPA), NAAPSA, and GTS. All these circuits have a point or playoff system to determine annual champions.

Regionals may be one-day events or may run for two or three days. Most feature the 5-player format, but 3-, 7-, and 10-player events are commonly part of the weekend festivities. Regional tourneys almost always are amateur-only events, but they are big enough to separate rookie, novice, and amateur players into different divisions.

Regionals typically draw from 25 to 75 teams. To keep the cost of travel down, each regional is designed to draw teams from an area encompassing a few states, rather than from all across the country. How many events each series holds in a year varies. Entry fees vary, but expect to pay more than for a local and less than for a national event.

Regional tournaments hold certain advantages compared with local events: They offer higher levels of organization, reffing, rules, and field layout. Regional events tend to be more relaxed and fun to attend than are the high-stress national events, but also much more competitive than local events. Regionals typically provide more games in an event than do the big nationals. And regionals almost always award more and better prizes and attract more industry vendors than do local events. Plus, the prestige of winning a regional (and potentially a circuit championship) is far more likely to bring a sponsorship to your team.

There are disadvantages, however, because regionals exclude or restrict the participation of pro players. The top pro teams don't attend, so your team will not get to play against them or see the equipment and tactics they use. The referees may not be as experienced as at the national events, resulting in some variations in judging calls. Also, regionals are more expensive to attend than are local tourneys because of travel expenses.

In summary, regional events are the middle ground of tournament paintball. The better regionals combine the best features of big national and small local tourneys.

From OP, to WORP, to TP, each transition brings more and better paintball. Tournament play isn't the end of the line; it's a new beginning.

Indoor Paintball

Jessica J. Sparks

"Behind you!" whispers your friend. You spin, eyes peering through the fog. Nothing. The lights flicker. Paint-splattered walls gleam in the dim light.

"I'm moving," you tell him. Every sense on overdrive, one hand on the wall, you crouch and move toward the door. What's there? Three steps later you leave the room. Another room. Dark shadows. Empty, you think. Around another corner you go.

Thwack! Thwack! Thwack! The wall beside you takes three hits. "Missed!" you call. Heart pounding, palms sweating, you pull back into the empty room. Thwack! Thwack! You spin, you duck, you move. Thwack! No time to think, just react. Thwack! Move. Move, to a dark corner behind a little barrier. "Who's shooting at me? My friend? Not my friend? Where? Now what?"

Enter another world. A world where safe danger awaits, often mere inches away. A world where lights and sounds can transform the familiar into the unreal. Welcome to indoor paintball.

Paintball started outdoors in the woods. Now, increasing numbers of entrepreneurs offer indoor paintball play to people living in the city. Indoor paintball brings the woods game to you. Why do people play paintball in the first place? Primarily, people like to shoot. Why play indoor paintball? The same reason. Paintball offers people a competitive shooting sport that has a good safety record. People of all ages can enjoy playing the game. Women and men compete equally. It's a whole lot of fun.

Differences

What's the difference between playing indoors and playing outdoors? Indoors, games run for shorter time periods. They usually last five to seven minutes, compared with outdoor games that usually last about 30 minutes. Sometimes an indoor field runs continuous games, where a tagged player leaves the game for three to five minutes and then may go back in.

Indoor paintball fields are usually closer to the players so there's less drive time. Shorter games indoors give players more games to play. Players spend less time waiting between games. The cost of a morning playing indoors is about the same or maybe a little less than the cost of half a day outdoors, but without the long drive. Some indoor fields offer air-conditioned playing courts, players' lounges, and changing rooms.

Tim Stone plays both indoor and outdoor paintball. He finds the indoor game sharpens his outdoor skills. "Indoors gets you used to moving when you have people close," Stone said. "Then when you go outdoors, it doesn't matter if you have trees or bushes instead of walls. The idea is that someone's close and you have to find a way to eliminate him or go around him. Indoor paintball teaches you how to deal with tight situations."

First-time indoor player Don Robinson said, "I realized the value of your team indoors. They let you know what's going on, except there are times you can't hear them because of the noise. Indoors is a lot noisier than outdoors."

Indoors, players wear old clothes. Jeans, a sweatshirt, and sneakers make a good outfit. It's recommended that players wear knee pads because the floors are usually concrete and often a bit slippery. Teams can wear football-style jerseys with players' names and numbers, particularly for tournament play.

Many indoor paintball tags happen "up close and personal." Since paintball tags can sting, players should protect themselves. Upper-body pro-

tection may be a rental vest with pockets for carrying your paintballs, or a motorcycle-style chest protector, such as those manufactured by JT USA. Male players are strongly advised to wear protective athletic cups. Gloves protect the hands, as in outdoor paintball. Full head-protection systems are mandatory.

Permitted paintball marker velocities vary indoors, but they are nearly always less than outdoor velocities. The speeds are reduced because a player may get tagged point-blank. Outdoors, fields generally permit velocities up to the industry standard for maximum permissible velocity, which is 300 feet per second (fps) for all paintballs of generally available commercial manufacture. Indoor field speed limits generally range from 200 to 250 fps. In very large indoor fields, where shooting distances can be as far as outdoor distances, velocities may be slightly higher than those at smaller indoor fields, but they must always remain within industry safety limits.

Players who are used to playing outdoors at 280 to 300 fps and find out they have to tune their paintguns down to 200 fps say, "The paintballs won't break." Not so. Today's paintballs are gelatin capsules filled with a nontoxic, noncaustic, biodegradable colored fill. They are like big vitamins. On impact, the gelatin splits open to leave the brightly colored fill. The gelatin will split open at speeds of 200 fps and slower. The paintguns work at those speeds, too.

Large, clear Plexiglas or strong safety-glass viewing windows or netting protect spectators at most indoor fields. Referees often control the games from elevated referee stands from which they can see the action. If a player needs a paintcheck, the referee can call the player "neutral," have the player step into the light with hands

Tournament competition indoors

up, spin for a check, and then put the player back into play—all without coming down to the floor. Floor referees can be directed to players who need to be checked by the refs above the floor.

Indoor paintball fields usually have a target range. A person or youngster not ready to play paintball can shoot at the target range. It might have moving targets. It might have a "Hogan's Alley" course, where targets (or real people wearing paintball masks) appear as the shooter moves through the course. The course can be a "shoot–don't shoot" scenario, with "good guys" and "bad guys" for targets.

Law enforcement benefits from indoor paintball fields. Police-training activities always include different kinds of building scenarios. Two common training scenarios involve rescuing hostages and finding suspects inside buildings. These scenarios can be run with paintball equipment very effectively. Indoor field operators generally offer local law enforcement free or reduced-fee use of the facility during the week for private training sessions.

New Trends

The newest trend for indoor fields is to hold arena-ball tournaments. Even an indoor facility with only one playing field can host these competitions. Formats are usually five-, three-, or two-player teams, or Top Gun, one-against-one. The concept for bunker arrangement often is to have mirror images on each side of the field, for balance, to let the skill of the players determine the outcome—as much as possible.

Opening an Indoor Field

With imagination and enough dollars a person can transform a warehouse, a movie theater, a barn, a grocery store, an airport hangar, or a former schoolhouse into a recreational paintball facility. In these times, when commercial property owners are happy to have tenants, many properties are being put to such novel sport uses by imaginative businesspersons.

Starting an indoor paintball field begins with finding the right building. The playing area should be large. How large? Ask yourself when you look at the actual playing area if you think it's big enough. The minimum size for a commercially viable operation appears to be 8,000 square feet. The building you choose can already have rooms or be empty, like a warehouse, since walls can be added or taken down. Each building needs careful evaluation. The more you know about construction, the better.

The next step is to find out what uses the land and building are zoned to permit. Zoning regulations are different in every city, county, and state, so the prospective field owner needs to check into zoning immediately. No lease or building purchase should occur until operating permits are assured. Paintball is most often played in areas with zoning that permits commercial recreational businesses, such as health clubs, tennis clubs, golf courses, and other such activities. Sometimes the zoning code permits paintball without any special permit. However, because paintball is so new, it usually is not covered by the zoning code. Often a "conditional use permit" must be obtained. This requires an application and an application fee, and often a hearing.

If the prospective field owner runs into a number of people who seem to be making it extraordinarily difficult to get a permit, it is best to hire an attorney early on. Zoning hearings are the places where paintball goes on trial. If you are serious about opening a field, and you are facing resistance and possible discrimination from neighboring business owners, landowners, or government officials, you need to get an attorney involved as soon as possible.

Practical matters to consider include windows (they have to be protected from paintballs and players who may trip), parking (you need enough to meet zoning regulations), the general area (properties in crime-ridden areas are inexpensive but your customers won't want to visit), lighting outdoors and indoors, cleanup (how do you intend to keep paintball splat cleaned off the walls and floors?), security, and so on. Every aspect of the business must be planned. How will you promote the field to corporations? Will you take credit cards? How much should you charge? What kind of paint will you order for the field? How many rental paintguns, and what kind, should you buy? In the planning stages, it's a good idea to get input from as many different, reliable sources as possible.

The most fun can be planning the inside of the building. Given your budget, what fantasy playland can you create? Will you have moveable walls? An electronic scoreboard? Exits all along the walls to make it easier for players to enter and leave the field? Fog machines? Ramps? Carpets or other types of flooring? Will you play music? It's all in your creative hands.

22

The Forty-Plus Player's Guide to Hardcore Paintball

Keith Fender

When my 22-year-old son Matt dragged me off to my first day of paintball, I thought "I'll do it just to keep my son happy." As the paintball bug bit me, though, I quickly found myself at the field whether or not my son came. I found that paintball fit with me in a way that no other sport or hobby ever had in the past. Paintball is a great excuse to be outside (with nothing to skin and clean). Also, you get to hang around with good people. Matt and I made paintball a weekly thing—and almost all we talked about.

Matt showed a real skill for the game. Local teams scouted him in a hurry, while I continued with the walk-ons. He played in multiple tournaments, while I became "Matt's Dad" and a fixture at tournament sidelines. As I watched these tournaments, I started to get this wild idea: While it is true, my combat boots are older than most of the players, I could be out there. I knew that I was not going to replace Bob Long for the Ironmen, but I knew I could hold my own.

Soon I hooked up with a group of guys of various ages from my local field. We started our own team with the idea of playing in tournaments and having as much fun as possible. We discovered a few facts of life that apply to the average geezer. A few minor adjustments must be made if a geezer wants a smooth transition from walk-on to tournament ball.

1. Get lots of paint. Your handy, old 100-round loader and 200 extra paintballs just won't cut it. You need to carry a lot more paint. This does not mean you need a $700 Auto-Hog with $300 worth of gear (but it helps and, hey, I am a grown-up now). It means only that you will shoot more paint now, and you will need to be able to

Let the young legs do the running!

carry it without dragging a cardboard box onto the field.

2. Get comfortable. "A man has to know his limitations." As a wise old sergeant told me in 1968, "Never walk when you can stand, never stand when you can sit, and never sit when you can lie down." When making game plans, it would be unwise for a geezer to say, "I'll sprint over to the tape on the other side of the creek." That is the job of some young buck with more stamina than sense. You are a geezer. Get *used* to it! Your job is to get to that *big* tree without falling down. Your job is to lay cover fire for that brave young soul making that quick dash. Paintball is best enjoyed on the field, not in the hospital. Know your limitations and play around them.

3. Keep your head. Most of the older players I know have an excellent field presence. We tend to stay in control and know what is going on around us, while the younger players scurry like rats from tree to tree. We seem to do well in the center where there is less running, more shooting, and where we are in the center of the game. Most younger players like to be on the tape. These two types of players really complement each other.

4. Be safe. Look, acknowledge the fact that you are not 20 years old any more, and that in addition to needing 'gun oil after a day's play, you also need some Ben-Gay and an ice pack or two. Know your limitations and play around them, but do not sell yourself short.

5. Have fun. Paintball is a game. Be sure that your teammates, and even your opponents, are having a good time. Remember, the younger players are watching you. Like it or not, you are setting an example for your kids and for many

Being a top competitor in paintball is independent of age.

other younger players. Keep your perspective, promote good sportsmanship, and show them how to have fun. Having fun is good for the game and everybody involved.

Having fun at paintball is independent of age or gender. It is a great setting for many unique and positive social interactions. Paintball is not just about winning, you know.

Age and treachery . . . will (sometimes) overcome youth and skill.

Quite a few professional paintball players are over 40.

The O-35 Club
Cowboy Bob

Long ago, back in paintball's dark 12-gram age, a group of players looked at each other. "How old are you?" said one. "Well, how old are you?" was the reply.

A little foot-shuffling and a few coughs later, it turned out all the guys were over 35. Some enterprising fellow, spurred no doubt by some aftergame Chardonnay, dubbed the bunch "The O-35 Club," meaning the Over-35 Club. A team motto quickly followed: "We don't run, we don't crawl, and we don't do hills." The penalty for running, crawling, or doing hills was immediate cries of "You buy the pizza!"

Only thing is, time marches on. The O-35 Club is now more aptly named the O-40 Club, and we're starting to wonder about a few who have nudged the big 50. Are we all still in the game? You betcha! The team's T-shirts read, "Age and Treachery Will Overcome Youth and Skill."

Competition
Paintball

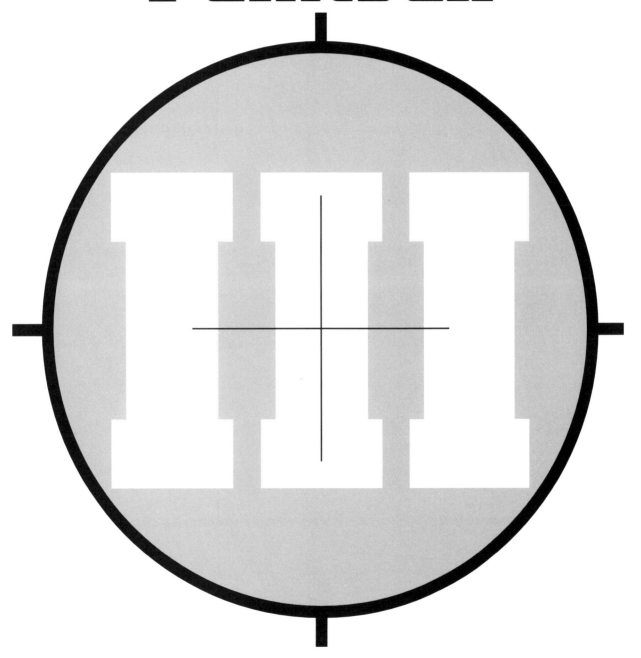

Twenty-One Tips for Those First-Tournament Jitters

"Thor"

Eventually, if you stay with the game long enough, you'll probably want to test your skills in a tournament. Tournament play can help you assess your strengths and weaknesses as an individual or as part of a team. Here are tips to help you survive that first tournament experience.

1. Stick close. Pick a tournament close to home. There's nothing worse than paying $600 or $700 to travel far away for your first tournament, only to find you didn't have such a great time.

2. Go for quality. Choose an event with a history of running safe tournaments with decent judging. An event that's had the same event producer for three or four years probably has the "bugs" worked out of it. Ask about the experience of the judges, such as whether the judges will be certified or from experienced teams. The judges have a strong effect on whether the event is a positive or negative experience.

3. Get the scoop. Get every possible bit of information about the tournament that you can. Cost is very important. Of course, you need to know the amount of the entry fee and whether you buy their paint or bring your own. Ask about a discount for prepaying for your paint. Do they accept personal checks or credit cards once you get to the event, or will you need cash or traveler's checks? How about air fills? Can you bring your own fill station, or do you rent one at the field?

4. Don't get lost. You need good directions to the field. If there is a hotel for the captains' meeting, get directions to it, too. You don't have to stay at the main hotel—and it might be more expensive, too, so check into that.

5. Creature comforts. Ask if there will be food, soda, and water available at the field. If not, bring your own.

6. Captains' meeting. Expect a captains' meeting. Be sure you know where and when it will be held. Take into account the time zones—perhaps you live in one zone and the event is in another. It's discouraging to show up 10 minutes early for the captains' meeting to find that it started 50 minutes before. The meeting may be held the night before the event starts or the morning of the event. Waivers and all money are usually due no later than at the meeting.

The Ultimate Judge usually runs the meeting, though it might be run by the event promoter or field operator. You are expected to have read the rules before you attend. The Ultimate will not go through each and every rule. There may be rules changes. Your schedule will be handed out. If you have a question about any of the rules, ask it when the Ultimate calls for questions. And call the Ultimate "sir" or "ma'am"— being polite does not hurt. Neither here nor at the field should you ever, ever argue with the Ultimate. You will lose the argument, and if you argue hard enough, you may find your team gets extra penalty points besides.

After the meeting, you may have time to talk to a few of the other captains. They will be sizing you up, asking you what your team is shooting, about your experience, and so forth. Listen more than you talk.

7. Rules. The team captain must get a copy of the event rules ahead of time. Give a copy to every player on your team. You are all responsible for knowing the rules.

Choose a spot with good cover and a clear field of fire.

8. Walk the fields. Get to the field the day before the event starts if at all possible. Everyone on the team needs to walk each field. If you can get a local player or staff member to show you around, that's good; ask for his or her opinion as to how the field plays and for any pointers. The person might feel it's unfair to help you, but you can explain it is your first tournament and the person might then be a little more helpful. The only stupid question is the one you do not ask.

Walk the fields from *both* flag stations. What looks like great cover from Station A may have a vulnerable spot from Station B. Take notes and make drawings. If possible, videotape the fields and comment as you tape (e.g., which field you are on, which station you are walking toward or from). You can take Polaroid pictures, too— whatever might help you make your game plans. Make a plan from each station. It's okay to talk to players from other teams whom you meet on the field, too. You can ask who they are, and who are the expected "favorites" for the tournament. Most teams will tell you about the competition, if they won't talk about themselves. You can ask which teams are likely to come at you and which are likely to sit.

Be friendly. You do not want to start your first tournament by getting the reputation of being a jerk. If you cop an attitude, the word will get around.

Be chrono'd and ready early.

9. Check your 'guns. You should check your paintball markers at the field on the day before the event starts. Shoot them, check for leaks, chrono them where you want them to be the next day. Whatever can go wrong with your 'gun at a tournament, will. The best-behaving, most reliable 'gun you have will suddenly blow an O-ring, refuse to come down in velocity, or blow paint, just because it knows you're at a tournament. (Take a spare 'gun.) Fill all tanks the day before the event starts. Do not rely on being able to get them filled the morning of the event. It might be cold and you could get cold fills and not chrono right. The fill stations might not be set up

if you are buying field air, or the line might be long, meaning you will get rushed and pressured —and you don't need any extra pressure.

10. Stay together the night before. The night before the event starts, keep the team together. Eat together. Look for other teams and watch how they're behaving. If they're loose and having a good time, they probably will have that kind of attitude at the field. Back at the motel, everyone needs to check his or her gear. Replace questionable lenses or seals. Do *not* shoot in your motel rooms, not even dry fire. You should have taken care of your 'guns at the field earlier in the day. Besides, the people in the next room might not understand what they are hearing, and they might complain to the management or even to the police. And do *not* wipe your 'guns and greasy 'gun parts on the motel towels and sheets.

Try to get nine hours of sleep. You won't get nine hours of sleep, of course, because of nerves and excitement, but at least you might get seven instead of four or five.

11. Game day. Load up and get ready to leave the motel. *Stop.* You have forgotten something. Send someone (or two someones) to check the room. Look under and in each bed. Look in the closets and the drawers. Look over the bathroom especially. It's a big disappointment to get to the field and discover your harness is hanging on the shower rod in the motel bathroom where you hung it to dry the night before after you washed out the old paint. Leave a tip for the maid, who will earn it.

Eat a light breakfast. You will have butterflies, and they will not fly as much if they are not standing on five pancakes and greasy bacon.

Game on!

Avoid coffee. You'd be surprised at how fast your stomach converts it to acid.

12. Staging area. There should be some designated place for your team to put its gear. Set up your table (if you brought one), your canopy (if you brought one), and have everyone start getting the gear ready. If the captains' meeting is held before the games start (rather than the night before), the captain has to attend. Have another player get the captain's gear reasonably ready while the captain goes to the meeting.

13. Be ready. Whenever your first game is, be ready. Be ready early. A late team may even forfeit a game.

14. At the flag. When you stand at the flag station for your first tournament game, your heart will race. Your blood pressure will rise. Your stomach will feel like you just swallowed a seagull. If anyone on your team says he's not going to faint or throw up, he's lying. You also will be

pumped. You will feel as if you could set a new world record in the 100-yard dash. *Stop.* If your team comes out of the box like greyhounds blindly chasing "BeeBee" around the track, expect to be maxed in less than three minutes. At least for the first game, just make the good cover spots you picked out when you walked the field. That's your best strategy against experienced opponents. They will expect you to be moving toward them with tunnel vision and knees knocking. Maybe you will lose, but you will stay in the game longer.

15. Win or lose. Here's a hard fact to accept. You probably will lose that first game. So what? You came here to learn. You wanted to test your abilities. The other teams may all be seasoned, experienced tournament teams. Play clean and do your best. After each game the captain checks with all his team and with the judges for any penalties and the score, and then signs the score sheet. Before score sheets are signed, the captain must confer with his players to see if any of them had an on-field problem that needs to be discussed. It is sad to say, but once in a great while an opponent will cheat. If this happened, the captain should take the matter up privately with the head judge for the field. Do not accuse without being sure you are right. Remember, to accuse is to challenge an opponent's reputation, so before you do this, think it through. The captain must stand up for the team, but you do not want to get the reputation of being a whiner at your first tournament.

16. Analysis. Between games, if you have time, see how your next opponent did. Try to talk to the team members that played them first and see if they will share any information about the game, and be willing to share information from

Use your team hand signals. Communicate!

your first game, too. Analyze what you did right and wrong in your first game. That does not mean pointing fingers and telling teammates that you got eliminated because of their mistakes. You are part of a team. If mistakes were made, the team made the mistakes. Stay with the positive things.

17. Communication. The most common mistake of new tournament teams is not communicating. Do not try to use complicated codes.

18. Mid-day. After your morning games, take a look at the scoreboard. If you are not in last place, it's more than you hoped for. Drink plenty of water. Eat a light lunch. Stay away from that coffee.

19. Afternoon games. It seems that many teams come out flat after lunch. Here's your chance to do better. Make sure your equipment is all ready, your 'guns are chrono'd, and you have plenty of paint and air. Go into the afternoon games with a positive attitude.

20. Good teams. By now you see that some teams are doing really well, while others aren't. Working as a team is what all the better teams do—and do well. Becoming a good team takes time and practice, and that does not mean getting out in the woods and playing against the same five people every other weekend. You have to go to tournaments and compete to get better at competing. Your head must be handed to you on occasion.

21. More attitude. Go out for every game with a positive attitude. Even if you do not score a point, you will still learn and improve as part of

Check the scoreboard throughout the tournament.

Stay with tournament play, and you, too,
will make the winner's circle.

a team. You will take home good memories. Recognize your flaws and work to correct them, but also recognize your strengths and build on them. At the end of the day, after the games, pick up all the trash from your area, whether or not it is yours. Thank the tournament organizer for having the event, and thank the staff and judges, too.

Remember, no one wins them all. Even the Ironmen lose one now and then. Don't get discouraged, and don't ever give up. Expect to crawl for a while, and eventually you may be running the flag in for the Big Win and that nice first-place trophy.

Play hard and play fair.

Cover and Movement

Russell Maynard

This article looks at how to combine using cover and movement to become a more effective player. In the opening move of a game, players run out from their flag station and try to get as far upfield as possible before they dive behind cover. What separates the good players from the mediocre ones is whether they choose effective bunkers to get behind. Just giving protection from the opposition's shots is not enough. If you can't shoot effectively from behind the bunker you pick, your position is worthless.

How many times have you watched a teammate make a spectacular dash to a bunker, only to get pinned down behind it? Since every player on the other team has a shot at his bunker, he can't expose as much as the tip of his barrel without being splattered. He picked the wrong bunker and overextended his position, and now his contribution to winning this game has become yelling for you to "Get them off me!" Not very effective paintball play.

Good players choose effective bunkers.

Underextending, stopping at a position too far back from the opposition, is safer but also ineffective. You have to pick a bunker that puts you close enough to the opposition for your shots to have an effect on the game. You may not be getting eliminations that way, but your shots pressure them, force them to duck behind cover, keep them from advancing or retreating to better positions.

Throughout a game you must adjust your position, moving from bunker to bunker, to stay effective. If you are about to become overextended, it's time to retreat. And when your current bunker no longer offers effective shots, it's time to advance.

Before You Move

Before moving from one position to another you must consider two factors: How exposed will I be while moving? How effective will I be once I get there? These two aspects, the amount of exposure and the effectiveness of a position, have to balance out. Is the risk worth the advantage?

First you must get an overview of the field. Determine which bunkers, if you could get to

Choose bunkers that give you effective shooting angles.

them, would give you the most effective angles of fire. Once you know where you want to go, look for ways to get there. Which opposing players will have a shot at you while you are moving? Are there lanes of cover you can move through? Figure out a step-by-step approach to get you from point A to point B before you move.

When You Move

The advantages of crawling are known. Fact is, most players prefer running to crawling. They feel more confident running from one bunker to another because it minimizes the time they are exposed as a target.

The disadvantage of running is that it increases the amount of exposure. When you run, your entire body is exposed. And while you are running, usually more than one opponent can see you and get a shot at you.

If you have to run from bunker to bunker, move laterally. A sideway-moving target is harder to hit than one moving directly forward or backward. Additionally, your lateral movement often encourages the opposing shooter to lean out from behind cover as he traces you with his paintgun. This makes it easier for your teammates to eliminate him.

Timing a Move

The timing of an advance from one bunker to another happens in two stages: First you, your teammates, or all of you have to distract or suppress opposing players who might have a shot at you. You need to get their attention focused some-

Move laterally when possible.

where else, so they aren't sighted in and prepared to shoot as soon as you expose yourself. The suppression can be direct (shoot at them until they duck behind cover) or indirect (draw their attention away from you, or away from the direction you will be moving).

The second stage of the advance is the movement. Be quick! Move fast! Stay low and go hard. Don't slow down until you are behind cover. You have to move without hesitation, but you also have to keep your awareness of the field. A really good

bunker player can run without losing sight of the target. Like a baseball player stealing a base, he or she takes a quick glance over the shoulder. An experienced player also relies on his or her ears.

Balls shot in your direction have a specific sound, and hearing the shots tells you a lot about range and direction. Maintaining field awareness with your eyes and ears as you run determines how you will finish up the move. If you don't see a player aiming at you and don't hear shots coming in your direction, it means you can slide into

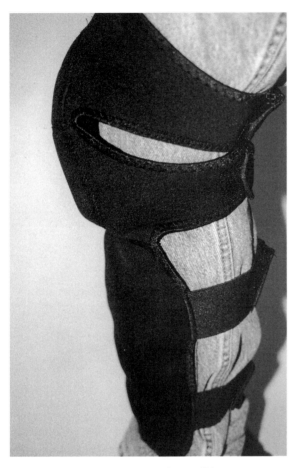

Wear protective gear if you're going to slide.

Make bunker moves ready to shoot.

cover, ready to shoot. If you hear shots and see players aiming at you, that means you need to get all the way behind cover and *hesitate* before sticking your paintgun out.

shoot around sides. By pushing up with your lower leg as you slide into cover, you can also pop up on one knee to shoot over the bunker. If you are being shot at and need to get as tight against the bunker as possible, just bend both knees and curl your torso when you slide. Take care—bunkers are notorious for having sticks, rocks, and other obstacles in the area where you would slide. The major disadvantage of head-first slides or dives is having to take one hand off your paintgun to brace yourself. Aiming is slower, and you can't get up into a kneeling position as quickly.

Finishing the Move

The most versatile way to finish a bunker run is with a feet-first, baseball-style slide. Lying on your back then with your legs extended toward the bunker, you can roll onto your left or right hip to

Summary

Practicing these cover and movement techniques will make you a better player. You will be a harder target to hit, and you will be a more effective member of your team during a firefight. Understanding the principles of cover and movement also will elevate your paintball strategies. Walking a field and preparing a game plan for your team takes on a new perspective when you recognize crawl lanes, effective bunkers, and all the other aspects of defensive and offensive positioning.

Practice playing in different sizes of bunkers.

2.5

Essential Tips for Better Team Practices

Jim "Roadrunner" Fox

A competitive tournament paintball team starts with the basics: players, gear, and a place to play. After that, it's time to practice. Tournament paintball is vastly different from walk-on play. The more intense the competition, the greater the difference. To prepare for tournament ball requires lots and lots of team practice.

Playing walk-on games can help your team improve, but only to a certain degree. You can work on communication, code words, and so forth, if you somehow can keep your entire team together amid the walk-ons—but it's not easy to do that. It's better to isolate your team on a field for a team practice. If you don't have a lot of experience on your team, do not hesitate to find one or two good, experienced tournament players to come out and help coach your team.

1. Scrimmages. Team practice days with other teams (scrimmages) are good to develop your skills. Have them come to your home field to practice, and trade off so you travel to their fields, too. The more teams from different fields you can hook up with, the better. This gets your team more familiar with different terrain and cover and how fields can be laid out. Meeting different (and sometimes unexpected) playing styles also teaches your team a lot.

2. Closed practice. You can also build your team's performance in a closed, team-only private practice. Here's where you develop your team's codes, talk strategy, learn new equipment, and especially get to know each other as teammates. You will be sharing motel rooms, meals, wins, and losses with your teammates, so you better get to be friends.

3. Targets. If you don't want to be shooting your teammates, set up cardboard or plywood

A scenario can be stopped for immediate coaching.

cutouts, simulating players, and set them throughout the playing field. Start a player or players from a flag station and have them work their way through the field. They drill by concentrating their multiple firepower on the targets, just as they would in a tournament.

Players can set up and shoot at the targets from different angles and shooting positions. They should crawl up on targets, shoot off-hand, pop up and shoot, and so on, just as if the target is a real opponent. It takes a little imagination (but not much) to do these kinds of drills. Practice with simulated targets helps make up for the hundreds of paintball games that newer players have not yet played.

4. Communication. Communicate all of the time. Communication is the key to winning. Work on using your team's code words to indicate the location of the target and to signal eliminated targets, pushes, and more.

5. Incoming. During drills, even with plywood cutouts as opponents, assign some players to add some incoming fire for realism. The idea is not to hammer your teammates who are drilling, but just to remind them to keep their heads down. The actual paintballs flying at them discourage the idea of staying up and away from cover too long to take extra shots.

6. Flags. You can incorporate flag pulls and hangs into the drills. You can have a player run a "gauntlet" of targets, where he has to locate and eliminate each target, proceed to get the pull, and make it back for the hang. When you do this, mix up the target positions or add extra targets to be eliminated for the return. Drills like this let you and your players see how accurate they are shooting and how good their field of vision is.

7. Conditioning. Endurance is important in a paintball game, just like in other sports. Those of you who have played football or baseball know what kinds of speed and endurance drills help with the legs. You may want to talk to a coach from these other sports and get help setting up drills for your team. These drills can get strenuous. Have all your players check with their personal physicians before getting involved in a training program.

8. Scenarios. In your private practice, the team coach or leaders can come up with different game situations to watch how your players adapt, react, anticipate, and improvise. You can play out any scenario or stop a scenario at any time for

Work on timed flag grabs during practices.

immediate coaching. Critique immediately after running a scenario for the benefit of the players; if you run several scenarios and then try to go back and discuss them, the players will not be sharp on remembering what happened in each one.

Throw different situations into each scenario. Have certain players run out of paint, have paintguns go down, use experienced players as referees giving tournament-style reffing. Be sure players know what to do (and what not to do) when a paintcheck is called on an opponent. They need to learn "quiet" ways to call a paintcheck on themselves.

When your team practices by itself, you can run these scenarios without shooting or with minimal paint shooting to keep the budget in line. Save your money for tournament paint.

Simulated game situations can be set up.

26
How to Use Codes

Nathan "Nobody" Greenman

My name is Tom. I'm the field captain on my team's left side. I can see the bunker right in front of me but I don't see anybody in it. My 'gun is going to stay pointed there until I'm sure. That bunker is the sweetest spot on the field and every smart team has someone there. Suddenly I see a hopper! The guy is shooting over the top instead of around the side of his cover. I get a clean shot on him. He doesn't yell "Out!" to let his teammates know he is out. Instead he just plugs his 'gun and walks away. "One in the box, one in the box!" I yell.

On my team's right side our captain is Pat. He makes it safely to his first position. So far he's been "long-balling" opponents. Pat hears me yelling, "One in the box, one in the box!" He yells back, "One in the box confirmed!" Now both sides of our team know we've taken out one opponent. Pat then yells, "Sixty-nine, sixty-nine!" This is the code we use when we want to push on a weak

side. Pat is saying he feels confident that he can hold his side and is offering to send his wingman over to me. He sends the man.

Now it's up to Pat to hold the right side at all costs. If Pat is taken out, our opponents can push through on Pat's wire and shoot the rest of us in the backside. If Pat should get hit, he must yell "Out!" very loudly so that the rest of the team can hear him. Back on the left side, the idea is for me (and whoever comes with me) to push on through the hole I made by taking out the opponents' wireman. If we do this, we should have the game in the bag. When I hear Pat's "Sixty-nine, sixty-nine!" it is my duty to call back "Sixty-nine confirmed!" Now I have the extra man, and it's time to charge.

"Blue, blue, blue!" is my next call. This code means everybody shoots. As soon as everyone is in position and fully loaded with paint, I get the confirmation from the rest of my players ("Blue,

blue, blue!"). We're all shooting to keep the remaining opposition down while we charge the left side.

The sound of five paintball guns throwing paint at the same time is awesome. Before the opponents knew what hit them, two of us were behind the other team. Game over. We had earned the points we needed to advance to the finals.

Why Codes?

Work on your team's codes. Codes do many things to help you win more games.

First, and most important, code usage forces you to develop teamwork. You must have someone listening if you are going to yell in the middle of a game. You must pay attention to your teammates if you're all using codes. Second, it can confuse your opponents and give you the element of surprise. You won't have to call out "Press the left now!" and let your opponents know what you are going to do. Say it in code. Hold the element of surprise. A split-second's hesitation can and will cost them the game.

I have witnessed one player hold off four by using codes. The four players did not keep track of the eliminations, so they didn't realize that there was only one player left on the other team. The one player kept yelling in code as if he were

talking to his own teammates (of course, he was the last one left from his team). It may seem funny, but it worked. The solo player kept his cool and used his head. He kept the other team confused and intimidated long enough to prevent their taking him out. He saved his team from getting maxed.

How to Talk in Code

Codes are part of what makes a team into a team. The codes should be easy for the team to use, and not so easy for the opponents to understand.

Numbers, simple number codes are used by nearly every team. Swarm's "Splash 1" or the Ironmen's famous call "G-1" mean the same thing: "We've eliminated the first one of our opponents." On the second elimination you hear "Splash 2" or "G-2."

How many players? Another way some teams have to use numbers is to call out "31," meaning "There are three of them in front of just little old me."

Codes are also used for zones. The field may be divided into sections, say, five sections across the field. If a player sees three opponents in the far left section, he would call "31," meaning three opponents in section 1.

How to Break and Defend Bunkers

Bart Schorsch

The paint flew so thick you could almost walk across it. Two of them made it out of the bunker. When they took out two of my buddies, I had my first revelation.

Look, I'm not really all that new to paintball. I've been playing for a couple of years, mostly outdoors in the woods with natural cover. A couple of hay bales or a really big tree were the closest thing to bunkers I'd ever seen. The day came to play at a field that had real building-style bunkers. I jumped at the chance: to shoot the turtles in the bunker, that is.

The game scenario put six in the bunker and ten outside. The team with the last survivor would win. Two stories high, the bunker had windows on three sides, a front door, plus an upper shooting platform that was quite exposed. The attackers had to cross an open field that did have decent cover around the edges.

Understand this about me: My usual game style is to sneak around in the bushes, hold a flank, and generally try not to be seen even by the people I shoot. The idea of nice captive targets made my trigger finger itch. What did my teammates think? It was like pulling impacted wisdom teeth from a pit bull to get any of them to volunteer to go inside the bunker. We all wanted to stay on the outside.

Our opponents started inside the bunker. We started across the field. As I said, I had my first revelation when two bunker-escapees clocked my teammates.

> *Revelation One: Don't let the people out of the bunker.*

Once you trap defenders in a bunker, don't let them out.

Keep 'Em In

Don't let the people out of the bunker.

If you *know* players are in a bunker, keep them there. The bunker restricts their field of fire. It's easier to count them when they're out. You can focus on the bunker, so you also have one less bush, bale, or barrel to watch.

After the initial flurry of shots slowed, the game settled down to steady shots. Both teams tried to work out who was where and then tag them. The fellow on top, on the shooting platform, worked into a steady rhythm of popping up, sniping, and dropping back down. His buddies inside the bunker spotted for him by looking through cracks in the walls.

Unfortunately, one of the relative newcomers on my team was also settling into a rhythm. He

and their top-side shooter both got tagged at about the same time. This led to revelations number two and number three.

> *Revelation Two: What a bunker lacks in mobility, it makes up in visual field.*
>
> *Revelation Three: Patterns are a bad thing.*

Visual Field

Odds are that a person in a bunker can keep an eye on a large area with little or no danger to himself. He can then spot for his buddies or another person. He also can be well protected while taking a shot.

A bunker usually gives solid cover.

But he does have to expose something in order to take a shot. Let's face it, a field owner could build a bunker full of tiny shooting ports, but what good would that be? There would always be a side or a window or a hole that someone would pop up and shoot from. If the opponent (or you!) developed a pattern in this popping up and shooting, one of you would be going to pop up just in time to take a hit. Vary your popping up and get used to paint flying just a few inches away from you.

Grenade

Our side was getting creamed by the porcupines in the bunker. I was desperate. I reached in my pocket and pulled out what my teammates refer to as "a Special," a paint grenade. This bunker was quite small, and other than a small upper ledge, it had no roof. I pictured a paint grenade sailing over the roof and the refs calling a bunch of them out. I got up on one knee and yanked the pin. Thinking of Gary Cooper, John Wayne, and Audie Murphy, I tossed the pineapple. Three things happened right away. First, I took a hit to the chest because I was stupid enough to rise up. Second, I saw the paint grenade go off a good 10 feet from the bunker. And, third, I had my fourth revelation.

Revelation Four: Get a plan ahead of time.

Be prepared to stay inside a bunker if you're going inside.

Get a Plan

If I had snuck up to another side of the bunker, my throw would have gone in, or maybe I would have splashed enough paint to get someone who was popping up. I should have waited to throw until I was closer, or I should have given the paint grenade to someone a bit less gung-ho. At the very least, I should have called for more covering fire from my teammates so I wouldn't have been tagged out.

Plug in, my 'gun high and mask on, my head low, I scampered from the field. I stood in the "observation zone" and watched the end of the game. When the referee finally called time, more defenders than attackers were left. The people in the bunker won. They won because the people outside the bunker had taken cover and then quit moving. The attackers might have had good cover, but the defenders had great cover. That is a recipe for disaster.

Revelation Five: If you aren't in a bunker, keep moving.

Fixed Place

The main disadvantage of a bunker or other fortified position is that it's fixed in place. You can't pick up the building and move it six feet to get a better shot on an attacker. The best thing an attacker can do? Don't try to out-bunker the bunker. Take advantage of your mobility and move in for a better shot! Otherwise you wind up with two teams taking turns shooting and ducking. Remember: The first encounter between naval ironclads (mobile bunkers!) wound up in a tied game. We decided to run the same scenario again. You bet I volunteered to be in the bunker!

Six of us crowded into the bunker and the referee counted down. One made it out the door, one jumped out a back window, and the shower of angry paint on the walls convinced the rest of us to stick around behind nice safe walls. One per-

When you use your bunker to the max, you can get great coverage.

A stand-up bunker helps you see farther.

cute tricks like lob a paint grenade or get you with a tricky angled shot. Put three or more people on the same person if you have to (making quick plans is much easier behind walls), and take the close people out. Even better, overlap your fields of fire and double-team an attacker.

I was spotting for a friend crouched at a smaller opening and taking pot shots myself when three things happened in very quick sequence:

1. The person on the ledge above us had his loader pop off and sail outside the bunker.
2. I ran out of air.
3. The guy I was spotting for ran out of air.

> *Revelation Seven: Bring lots of paint and air.*

son got up on the upper platform and began to hammer the other team.

I quickly found out that the increased vision in a bunker is a great thing. But this bunker had great big windows in it that didn't look so big when I was on the other side of the field. On this side of the wall, they definitely looked huge. I was zeroing in on a guy who was trying to creep closer, when I had revelation six.

> *Revelation Six: In a bunker, distance is your friend.*

Distance

The farther away you can keep the other team, the better. It's when they get close that they can do

Paint and Air

I pulled my spare ammo and passed it up above. The person did fairly well loading his marker "Gettysburg style," one or two balls at a time. After the game I asked around, and nobody had noticed that his loader was gone. Perhaps it made him more conservative in his shots.

Bringing more air and paint is a good idea no matter what kind of game you are playing, but in a bunker game, if nobody else in the bunker has brought extra paint or air, you have nowhere left to go. You can't fall back and regroup or borrow from anyone except your bunkermates. Suddenly down to two-and-a-half effectives (one inside the bunker, one outside the bunker, and one above, shooting rather infrequently), one of the outside

A scenario field offers many kinds of bunkers.

Inflatable bunkers are the hot ticket in speedball arenas.

that I was tagged and coming out, I had my final revelation.

> *Revelation Eight: Even a useless player in a bunker can still help the team.*

folks having been tagged out, the situation looked grim. Did we give up? Heck, no! Safely behind walls, I continued to spot and stick my head out the door to draw fire. I tried to make myself enough of a juicy target to entice people to break their cover. I was also taunting the enemy with juicy epithets. Not wanting to incur the wrath of the refs, I kept it to things like, "Grandma! Are you out there shooting?" and "We got 'em now boys! They can't hit a barn!"

After tempting fate like that, of course, I was hit in the head and declared out. As I yelled

Before I was hit, I had "shared out" my paint (field rules allowed this). And although my teammates were not able to tag anyone because of my taunts or exposing myself to incoming paint, they were able to get a good idea of where the other team was hiding. I trudged off the field and watched my teammates get tagged out before time was called. We were eager to go again (after getting air and paint), but the weather didn't cooperate. It began to rain.

My education in bunkers and structures came at a high price. But I paid it in full and even congratulated the people who had tagged me out. In the next game at that field I know exactly where I'm going to be. In the bunker!

Taking Bunkers

Jim "Roadrunner" Fox

Bunkers. The name sounds like trouble. Opponents hide in bunkers. Bunkers offer opponents nice cover and a nice ambush spot. Here's "bunker handling made easy."

A bunker in paintball is any kind of fortification (foxhole, hut, pallet, building, tower, wood pile, etc.). It may be camouflaged, in the open, or in brush. If an opponent is in that bunker, odds are he is going to see you before you see him. Even with a bunker that's out in bright sunlight, the opponent will sit quietly and lure you in. He is waiting for a close, good shot.

Bunkers often come in pairs. Look for supporting bunkers near the first one you find. Is it full or empty? When you first come upon a bunker, you have to ask yourself whether an opponent is in the bunker. You always have to assume that the bunker is occupied. The size and shape of the bunker can give you an idea of how many opponents might be in it. Usually there are one to three opponents in a bunker unless it is unusually large. Take into consideration how many people are on the opposing team and how much of the field they have to cover, and that may also give you a feeling for how many players they would want to send to the bunker.

A bunker is usually designed to give the person in the bunker several options. He or she may shoot over the top of the bunker. Most bunkers have shooting holes in the middle and sides, too. The opponent could be standing, kneeling, or lying down. He or she may come out around the side of the bunker.

To count opponents, look for paintgun barrels or for a bit of white CO_2 coming out of the barrels. Listen to the sounds from the bunker. Voices and the paintguns' popping will give you clues. It is also important to figure out the direction the opponent is facing because you will want to flank him or her if possible. Remember, you can be fooled by opponents who are in the bunker but do not shoot. You may even eliminate one opponent and think the bunker is empty. As soon as you step into the open, a hidden opponent can tag you out.

When you come upon a bunker, it is best to work with at least one teammate. You each approach the bunker from different angles. That means you have at least two angles from which to look inside the bunker and two angles from which to shoot into the bunker. Here's where it is important to know which way the opponent is facing. Yes, he can move, but if he is shooting at you, then your teammate can come in from another angle. Odds are your teammate will eliminate that opponent because he or she will be watching you and shooting at you.

The more teammates you have, the easier it is to take a bunker. One or more of you shoot paint to suppress anyone in the bunker. Your teammates work their way closer to the bunker, or work in from different angles, until they can eliminate the opponents.

Special Tips

1. Players will sometimes hide in bunkers to clean their paintguns, or to reload paint.

2. A bunker near a flag is nearly always guarded.

3. Bunkers will be scattered throughout the field, sometimes in unexpected places.

4. You may want to bypass a bunker if taking the bunker is likely to delay your squad too long in its quest for a flag capture.

5. If you do bypass the bunker, have one player watch the bunker so no one comes out of it and backdoors your squad.

6. Never fear taking the bunker. Look on it as a challenge.

7. You are taking on two things, the players and the fortification. One cannot move and the others can.

8. Taking a bunker requires time, practice, teamwork, communication, and the confidence that you can indeed take that bunker.

28
Patience and Discipline

Jim "Roadrunner" Fox

The two most important attributes you need in your game are patience and discipline. Patience refers to waiting out an opposing team or player. Your patience may make the difference in whether your team wins or loses. How to be patient is something you can learn from more experienced players. You learn when and why to be patient simply by playing, but that also means a lot of your learning comes from making mistakes. It's better to think ahead and learn from others' experience.

For example, patience can mean waiting for someone on the other team to do something stupid. A player might get careless and leave a foot or a loader sticking out the side of a bunker. When this happens, the player leaves himself exposed for a clean shot. Sometimes a player focuses too much on shooting to his right, and leaves his teammate facing a two-on-one over to

his left side. That's when you and your teammates can take advantage of the situation. Eliminate an opponent and take advantage of what you have earned. Then you may be able to make a push.

There will be several times during a game when you should be patient. There will also be times when you have been patient and then need to be aggressive, either by moving or opening fire on your opponents. In short, patience is followed by aggression. It's like the chicken and the egg thing, though. You may need just three seconds of patience—or nearly the whole game's worth. Your opportunities will come and maybe even go.

The secret is to develop a keen sense of the game so that you recognize the opportunities your patience has earned you. Learning to be patient and to balance that with aggression takes time. Stay with it. Getting impatient and discouraged is a quick ticket to the spectators' area.

169

Patient players open up at the right moment.

Discipline and patience go hand in hand. It takes discipline to wait patiently for that good, clean shot. Your shooting too early and missing often tells the opponent to pull that foot or loader in, where you won't get another clean shot. When you're being pressed by advancing opponents, it takes discipline and patience to wait until they are close. If you take that 45-yard shot, you're likely to miss and make them more careful; even if you do hit someone, the ball probably will bounce. But if you wait until they're in decent range, odds are you'll take one or more of them out.

You need team discipline, too, to keep everyone handling an assigned lane. If you are assigned to a wire, for example, you can't leave your assigned position without a very, very good reason. If you are always jumping up from your assigned position and running to the other side of the field because "nothing's happening" where you are, you won't be where your captain needs you to be. Players are sent to first positions for a reason, to give your push squad the time to crush the other side of the opponents' line. Listen to your captain.

Follow patience with aggression, when the time is right.

Discipline calls on you not to rush a player alone, and not to leave yourself exposed for a long period of time. Work with your team. You may need to be patient a few seconds extra while your teammate loads so he can cover you, but have the discipline to do that. When you are in a one-on-one situation, have the discipline to size up the situation and decide on the best route with *sufficient cover* so you can flank your opponent. Look to see which way your opponent shoots, left or right or over the top of a bunker, so you increase the odds of catching him looking the other way. See if he keeps coming out of his cover at the same time and from the same position, so you can pick him off.

You have to discipline your thought processes to analyze the situation you face. You must have patience to go through the thought process before you move. The more you work on this, the faster you will figure out the situation and the more instinctively you will make the right moves. Add patience and discipline to your bag of player skills. You will enhance your skills, and your overall level of play will rise to new heights.

Move not too soon and not too late.

Patience and discipline pay off with more flags.

Make all your opponents "go home," and you win the game.

29
Heroes and Zeroes

Cleo Sedlacek

"**H**eroes or Zeroes. Let's just do it!" That's what team Bango Tango was thinking as it headed into its championship game against team Next Level at the Skirmish Five-Man Classic.

The game was played on the Arena, Skirmish's showcase speedball court. The Arena has a diamond shape. Usually the team that controls the corners wins the game. When the whistle blew in this particular game, Bango Tango captain Dave Barndt and Leon Miller dashed for the corners. If they got shot, Brian Barno and Ken VanBuskirk would be right behind them. But the first two guys made it, allowing them to control the field, and two minutes later their back man, Joe Reed, hung the flag to win the game. The title went to Bango Tango.

What was Bango Tango's secret to winding its way through the other 23 teams to get to the championship game? A big element in this particular

tournament was climate control for their 'guns and paint. There was a solid coating of snow and ice on the field, and the temperature high was only in the mid-20s. It wasn't quite like playing paintball at the North Pole, but it was close enough to make things difficult for the unprepared.

Bango Tango kept two vehicles running all day long. They took their paint out only as they needed it, and they put their 'guns right back into the vehicles when they weren't using them. Consequently, team captain Dave Barndt said, he never broke a ball, and his 'gun worked well all day.

This was the 12th year for the Skirmish Fall Five-Man. The event has built up a following among established teams because of the guarantee of lots of games on interesting fields with good, solid judging. It also traditionally attracts several brand-new recreational teams (from Skirmish's huge mailing list) that get a chance to see what tournament play is all about. The new teams keep things interesting because they have no idea what the established methods of playing tournament ball are. You can expect just about anything from them.

Paintguns used in the tournament ranged from Skirmish's rental Automags to Trracers, Spyders, Tippmann Pro Lites, Minimags, Automag RTs, and Autocockers. Clothing varied from white T-shirts to urban camo, Renegade, JT jerseys, and a variety of woods camos. A female on a new team wore "body armor." At least one vinyl poncho was spotted. Tourney paint was excellent-performing RP Scherer Polar Ice.

Skirmish chose 6 of their 40 fields to host the multiteam event. Woods fields included Heart of Darkness 1 and 2, Creeper, and Fox. The two speedball courts were the Alamo and the Arena. The Arena is a colorful field that's netted and constructed with blue and white plastic barricades. It was a struggle to keep Skirmish's 400 rec players off the Arena for the day. It's the kind of field that looks cool to play, and they kept asking to play it. The Alamo was designed with a central tower and several outlying structures to be played as an offense-defense format. For a tournament, teams on the field start at either end of the structures.

Creeper is a basic woods field, beefed up with some strategically placed bunkers. Fox is also a woods field, about a third of it covered with the thick rhododendron bushes that make Skirmish famous and make for some interesting cover and hide-and-seek possibilities. Heart of Darkness is a woods-and-rhododendron combination that plays well for large groups of rec players. For the tournament, it was chopped into two fields to encourage faster action.

The 25-degree temperatures and a center-flag format also encouraged aggressive play. Even rookie teams, which might have tried to sit back under other conditions, played as fast and as hard as they could. A lot of players used the crust of ice underfoot to slide into bunkers, adding to the general excitement.

After six hours of rocking and rolling paintball, the three divisions of eight had finished their round-robin preliminaries, and single-elimination semifinals were set to begin. The teams that advanced were Bango Tango, Secret Agents, and Next Level as division winners, and Rapid Fire White, the wild card. Bango Tango beat Rapid Fire White, and Next Level took out Secret Agents, to set up the championship game on the Arena.

Skirmish handed out $500 to the first-place team, $300 for the second, and $200 for the third. The first- through fourth-place teams each got five individual trophies. Tournament Director Bruce Green said, "We finished in the daylight, it only snowed a little, and it never rained once. It was definitely a successful tournament."

These teams entered: Bango Tango, PA; Bass, PA; Camo Sharks, NY; Challenge Paintball, NJ; Check Mate, WV; Cobra, NJ; Dirty Devils, PA; Eliminators, PA; F-Troop, PA; Friendly Fire, NY; Gary's Guerrillas, PA; Olof's Berzerkers, NY; Rapid Fire Red, NJ; Rapid Fire White, NJ; Resolution, NJ; Ron's Team, PA; Shadow, NJ; Spartans, PA; Team Justice, NY.

30

My First Tournament
A Teen's Perspective

Nathan deKieffer

Before I relate the story of a first tournament through the eyes of a 16-year-old, I'd like to tell you a little about myself. I have been playing paintball since I was 11. My dad introduced me to this game. Paintball has been kind of a father-son bonding thing, but I think Dad likes the bonding more than I do.

Anyway, let me continue. I joined the Green Machine on my 16th birthday. The guys on the team shot me a couple of times for fun and then said I was "in." I had been practicing with them for about a year, so I was used to the drills, the codes, and the penalties for breaking the rules, but I had never been to a tournament.

My luck changed at the end of the month. The All-Americans were putting on a five-man tournament at Sgt. York's Friendly War Games in Pennsylvania. The Green Machine already had two five-man teams going up, but we had no alternates.

My dad signed me up, for the "experience," but he told me I might not play. I was still thrilled to go. The team left Saturday morning for the Sunday tournament, but I had other obligations (e.g., chores mandated by my parents and other activities of that caliber) so I couldn't leave until that afternoon. During the three-hour drive to Sgt. York's, I had to listen to my dad lecture about every single rule in the book and all the circumstances he'd encountered for the last 10 years as a player and judge.

I nodded and smiled every now and then to make my dad think that I was paying attention, but I was too excited about the tourney.

Upon arrival at our classy motel (it had a flush toilet and running water, hence "classy"), we saw three other players who had been running the fields. We asked them how the fields looked. They all spoke, each interrupting the other at every

175

sentence. I gave up trying to understand them after about five minutes.

Walk the Fields

They left. We threw all our stuff into our room, and my dad and I took off for the fields. When we got there, everyone was leaving. A couple of our teammates informed us that we were too late to look at the fields, and asked us to join them for dinner.

Dinner Tactics

We accepted, and at the thought of food, I became hungry (I'm not fat at 5 feet 11 inches and 145 pounds, but I can pack away a healthy portion). Half of our team went to one place and half to another. One of the halves rode off into the sunset and I didn't see them again until the next day. Our half sat together at a couple of tables pushed together, members discussing tactics for each field. They told me there were five fields, all level, with an incredibly large embankment on one side that overlooked the entire field.

The tactics we would use were fairly basic. The team went over certain special moves and how to handle possible situations.

Lights Out

With a bellyful of steak and a brain full of info, I left with my dad for the hotel room. We got there at 8:30 P.M. By 9:00, my dad was asleep. (At home, he is usually asleep around 8:30; he must have been too excited to sleep.) Just after Dad fell

asleep, one of my teammates, Pat, came around and checked on us and pretty much ordered me to be in bed by 9:30. He said almost everyone else was already in bed and that I should get a good night's rest.

After Pat left, I finished getting my gear together. Then I settled down to do some of my homework, which was due on Monday. After about five minutes, I figured out it was no use to try to concentrate on proving two lines were parallel or solving for x with complex conjugate roots when I had paintball on the brain. I went to sleep.

Five-thirty A.M. Already? I felt as if I had only been asleep for 10 minutes when my dad woke me up.

"Come on, son, it's already 5:30, our first game is at eight."

The words "already 5:30" replayed in my mind, and I laughed at the thought of my getting out of bed at this hour. To my surprise, I managed to get up, shower, dress, and make it to the car by 6:00. (If I were this excited for school, maybe I would be awake for the first four periods and not get as many detentions for sleeping in class.)

We pulled into the paintball parking lot a little before 7:00 A.M., after stopping for a quick breakfast. I was surprised that most players were already there and ready to play. We parked with the rest of the team and started getting our gear ready, operating out of the back of our "OJ" Bronco (yes, it is white and the same model and size and, yes, blood red is the color of our interior).

Captains' Meeting

At 7:00 the captains' meeting started. Even though I wasn't a captain, I went to hear all the rules (going was an edict from my paternal unit). The rules were nearly all plain and simple things I was used to hearing. I was really surprised how severe the penalty was for wiping or not calling yourself out when you were hit. For doing either of these, the refs would take you out and also pull out your two closest teammates, or, if your team didn't have two guys to be taken out, brutal penalty points would be assessed.

After hearing this, I was a little nervous. Don't get me wrong, I'm a fair player, but I worried about getting hit in the back bottle or someplace where you can't feel it very well. I was not used to calling a paintcheck on myself, but I imprinted into my brain that, today, if there was any doubt, I would have to call for one.

Nervous?

I was getting really nervous and anxious to play, but I had a feeling in the back of my head that I would not get to play because I was an alternate. I tried to assure myself that I would get to play.

First Game

When the first game rolled around, my 'gun was shooting around 350 fps, very hot. I dismantled it, looking for the problem. I didn't know that one of my other teammates, Walter, had the same problem. My 'gun was sitting in lots of pieces when my captain, Pat, asked if I could play. I was willing to go out without a 'gun, but they took someone else. When I finally got my 'gun under control, the game had started. I kicked myself because I should have been ready. Walter was ready by the second game and was able to play for the rest of the day.

Both of our teams jumped out to an early lead. With us battling for the top of the division, my chances of playing became bleaker.

A Chance to Play

Only when our Red Team bombed the fourth and fifth games, and it was pretty obvious that they could no longer place in the top two, did my turn come to perform. By the time I got on the field, I had been waiting to play for nearly six hours. When I stepped onto the field I was incredibly nervous and shaking with excitement. My mind kept relaying the messages "When in doubt, call for a paintcheck" and "Don't get hit." The whistle blew. I sprinted to my assigned position and scanned the area ahead of me. I spotted two opponents about 40 yards away. They were a little out of range, but I opened up anyway. My paint landed around them with no effect.

Eyes Up

I reached into my pack and grabbed a guppy to reload. Pouring in the contents, I kept my eyes ahead as I was supposed to do. When I reached for another guppy, though, I let my eyes down for a second. I didn't see a guy move up. He unloaded on me. I squirmed behind my tree, but it was too late, and I caught one right in the front of my loader. After checking the splat, I called myself out. One of the refs removed my armband, and I hurried off the field, grumbling at myself for making an incredibly stupid error. I vowed to make up for it.

When I got off the field, my dad, as a great loving parent, told me it was okay because I tried my best. I gave him a weak smile and said, "Thanks, Dad . . ." Under my breath, I completed my sentence with ". . . for the great encouragement, I really appreciate it; you can go away now." We lost the game, but not only due to my rookie mistake. We made other mistakes. Mainly, our communication from the beginning was lost, and that brought about our downfall.

Splatter City

Walking to the field for my second game, I reminded myself to play my best and not get hit. I did a lot better than in my first game. About halfway through the second game, I was pinned down behind a flimsy bunker and my 'gun was totally messed. Fiddling with it and trying to dodge paintballs, I managed not to get hit for a long time. Then the game turned into a three-on-one (me being the one).

They splattered me beyond belief. A ref stood over me as I kept getting splattered. I kept on asking for a paintcheck. Each time, to my surprise, the ref told me, "You're clean!" I had enough white splatter on me to pass for a snowman. With about a minute to go, they finally snuck one in and caught me on the top of my head. Stumbling off the field, trying to see through my now opaque lenses, I saw the other team grab the flag and hang it. I knew I had only one more game to prove myself.

Last Chance

Back at our car, I used a roll of paper towels to clean myself off and restore my camo, 'gun, and goggles to their original color. The team let my dad and me play together for this last game. Dan

also gave me his 68-Automag to play this game. Preparing to play, I told myself that this was my last chance to be a hero.

At the field we drew up our tactics. Chris would take the hill, my dad to his left, me in the middle, Mark to my right, and Gary to go swimming in the creek. All set. The whistle blew. I raced to my assigned tree. I looked into the darkness of the woods ahead but didn't see anything. Mark moved up and I joined him.

Then I saw the flag about 15 yards away. Above that was the hill with Chris at the top in a firefight against two guys. My dad moved up with Chris, and they shot one of the guys at the top. I yelled to my dad, "Cover me!" I raced for the flag. I heard their guy at the top yelling, "He's got the flag! He's got the *flag*!" I grabbed the flag—but I grabbed both sides of the flag so when I jerked it, it didn't budge! I grabbed again, with the same results.

I grabbed a third time, this time making sure I only grabbed one side. Pulling the flag free, I dived into cover while paint danced all around me. Chris and my dad hosed the guy who was shooting at me. Meanwhile, Gary had gone up the creek, shot two guys, and was in a firefight with another in their station. Mark was already out.

When the shooting stopped and I heard Gary calling that he had just got another kill, I ran in and hung the flag. After checking me, the ref blew the whistle, and I had a smile embedded in my face that plastic surgery couldn't have removed.

Walking back to my cheering teammates, I said it was nothing and tried not to let my ego get too big. While I was trying to suppress my ego, the rest of the team was ragging on my dad for being so cheap and not letting me have a 'Mag. After "chrono'ing" off, I felt as if I was walking on air. My first tournament ever, and I had got a flag grab and proved myself to my teammates.

Dad

On the drive home, my dad said, "I'm proud of you, son; you did your best. You did it without anyone telling you . . ." This time I let him talk and actually listened for a change.

Epilogue

My dad finally did back down and get me my Automag; I had to pay half the cost. I am still on the Green Machine team. I slept well that night after the tournament.

I didn't end up finishing my math homework, and I got detention the next day at school for not doing it. I also got detention for sleeping during class.

Advanced Tactics
Formations

Russell Maynard

The skirmish line is the basic formation of tournament paintball. It's the only formation most teams know and use. Game after game, whether they win or lose, nine of ten teams do the same thing: Their opening move is to send one player to each side boundary to take positions behind the best available bunkers. Meanwhile the three other players on a five-man team spread out and advance up the field until they reach cover positions more or less on a line between their two boundary teammates. Sometimes one player (usually the captain) stays back from the skirmish line to act as a reserve. His job is to move from side to side and fill in any gaps that form as the skirmish line attacks or defends.

Once the skirmish line is established, the game proceeds like a couple of heavyweights slugging it out face-to-face. Both sides hug their bunkers and pound out the paint. There's plenty of shooting and

The skirmish line puts all your team's firepower up front.

shouting but very little maneuvering. The major advantage of the skirmish-line formation is its brute force. A skirmish line puts all your team's firepower up front against the opposition, setting up a wall of paint from boundary to boundary. If your team's firepower is more effective than theirs and you can get up by one or two eliminations, then your team will try to push forward through the opponents' skirmish line and flank their remaining players.

The skirmish-line formation works great against players who are less aggressive or can't shoot as fast and accurately as your team (which is why it seems to be such an effective formation to new tournament players with high-tech 'guns who are used to going against walk-ons with rentals). But when new teams start playing in major tournaments against equally armed and aggressive competition, they soon experience the skirmish line's disadvantages.

If the other team's firepower is as strong and accurate as your firepower is, and their bunkers give them as much protection as yours does, then the game turns into a stalemate. Both teams are stuck in positions from which they can't advance or retreat, and their midgame strategies have been reduced to "Stay alive, save some paint, and hope the other side makes a mistake." It's like WWI trench warfare: Between the two skirmish lines is a neutral area, a no-man's-land into which one team or the other will have to charge if it wants to try for a flag pull to get some points.

Because most tournament teams rely on the skirmish-line formation, most games between evenly matched teams are stalemates until the last minute of play. Then, with the clock ticking down, one or the other or both teams rush out into the neutral area hoping to get lucky (lucky breaks on "them" and lucky bounces off "us").

The job of the pointman is to push forward.

And, of course, both sides are hoping, praying, and arguing for all the ref calls to go their way.

Advanced Formations

Experienced, tactically intelligent teams understand the limitations of the skirmish-line formation. They don't like stalemated games that turn into middle-of-the-field melees as time is running out. They don't like having to rely on lucky hits, lucky bounces, and refs making difficult calls to decide who wins critical games. They know from bitter experience that using the skirmish-line formation is the root cause of all these potential problems and uncertainties, and they've learned the best solution is to move beyond the skirmish line to more advanced formations.

Tactically advanced teams prefer a staggered formation to the skirmish line. Offensively, a staggered formation can penetrate into the neutral area better than can a skirmish line. Defensively, a staggered formation is much harder to break through and flank. And both offensively and defensively, the staggered formation offers much more team maneuverability.

A staggered formation positions players on a five-man team into a **W** or an **M** arrangement. The **W** formation has three players up front and two in the back. The **M** formation puts two forward, two back, and holds one in reserve in the middle. Both formations are based on the interaction of two two-player squads working as subunits within the team.

Pointman–Wingman

The two-player squad functions in a pointman-wingman formation. The job of the pointman is to push forward. His goal is to advance to a position from where he has a better shooting angle at a target or from where he can initiate a tactical play. The job of the wingman is to protect and support the pointman while he is moving into position, then make the secondary move of the tactical play.

The roles of the two players often change and flip-flop as the game situation develops. If the wingman sees an open lane and dashes or crawls to a position beyond his partner's, then he becomes the pointman and the original pointman becomes his wingman. Each time they leapfrog past each

The wingmen suppress as the pointmen advance.

other, their jobs and responsibilities switch. The player up front might have to pop up and suppress a bunker to enable his backup to move forward.

Spacing

Maintaining the correct gap or spacing between the pointman and wingman is critical to the efficiency of this formation. The wingman has to stay close enough to protect his pointman, that is, to shoot anyone who charges out and tries to bunker his partner. The wingman also must stay within range of, and have a good shooting line at, the bunker or bunkers in front of his pointman. If the wingman can't suppress those players, his pointman can't advance on them. So every time the pointman moves up to a new cover position, the wingman also should move forward to the next cover position. Good two-man teams seem to move simultaneously.

Looking at the other side of the coin, their staggered formation will deteriorate into a skirmish line if the wingman closes the gap too much and ends up next to his pointman. They will lose their ability to maneuver, and their push will stall out. Don't ever forget that two or more players behind the same bunker or in the same shooting lane can be suppressed as easily as one can be.

Middleman

On a five-man team using the staggered formation, the middleman has several roles to play. At the start of the game he might have to push forward and lend firepower to establish and control the neutral area between the two teams. As the game progresses, he might have to replace an eliminated player in one or the other pointman-

wingman squads. The ideal situation is when the middleman can stay back, uncommitted until his team is ready to run their midgame play. Having stayed back, he is free to maneuver left or right and join up with one or the other squad.

The pointman-wingman formation changes when the middleman joins in on the attack. Typically the forward-and-back distances between the pointman, wingman, and middleman will lessen or close as they push up the field and spread apart to increase the width of their shooting angles. As the attack penetrates past the other team's line, one of the three players (usually whoever is farthest back in relationship to the direction of the charge) becomes the "trailer," whose job is to follow behind his teammates and clean out any opposition that tries to stop the flanking. The opposing players who turn and come out of their bunkers to try to shoot the flankers are easy targets for the trailer.

Ten-Player Teams

We've concentrated here on the two-man squad as the basic subunit within a five-player team's staggered formation. But most of the ten-player teams who use a staggered-line formation prefer three-man squads made up of one pointman and two supporting wingmen. With twice as many bodies on each side and a whole lot more paint flying around the field, the pointman needs twice as much support and protection to penetrate into the neutral area. Some ten-player teams set up their three-man squads in right, left, and middle divisions, with one player held in reserve. Other teams like to run three-man squads on each wire with two two-man squads filling in the middle.

Summary

If you're tired of the same old routine and same limited results from using the skirmish-line formation, maybe it's time for your team to move on to more advanced formations, such as the staggered line. The beauty of the staggered line is that it offers a lot more maneuverability, which means a lot more variety. Why not try it? You and your teammates might like it.

Tricks of the Game

Jim "Roadrunner" Fox

Every game, every sport, has its inconveniences. Paintball is no exception. However, if you think of these inconveniences as challenges to overcome, and then overcome them, you will become a better player. Here are a few of paintball's challenges—and ways to help you triumph over their adversity.

On the Field

Many challenges besides dodging paint and making the right moves await a player. The game, though it is simple, becomes more complex (as does chess, baseball, bowling, or any other sport) the more you play it. Here are some common challenges you are likely to encounter.

- Being called out of a game for an old hit that you just forgot to clean off between games is

a major inconvenience. Check yourself and other teammates after a game for broken paint. Clean off all the old hits. I'll describe a way to do this later.

- Speaking of being called out when you weren't hit, remember when you move to a position on the field to find a second or two to look at the ground and the barricade, tree, or rock you're now behind. You usually can find broken and unbroken paintballs in the area if you're playing on a field that gets a reasonable amount of action. You should brush this mess away from the location where you have positioned yourself. Otherwise, you may kneel on a paintball or on paintball fill. In a tourney, you would want to call a ref over to see what you're doing (and to see that, no, you didn't get hit on your hand where there's some fill because you brushed the mess away). If you find that you

When you take a position, it is a good idea to clear broken and unbroken paintballs from your location so you don't kneel on one. Let a ref know what you are doing.

have knelt on a paintball and it breaks, do not move and do not try to wipe the paint off. Call a referee over to your position and explain to him or her what has happened. The referee will instruct you on what to do. Good referees know the difference between a hit and a knelt-on paintball and they will allow you to remain in the game.

Your staging-area routine should include a check that you have a full tank and full paint pods at the start of each game.

- If you lean against a barricade or tree and get paint on you that might later be confused with a hit, call a referee over and show him or her what happened.

- In a tournament always check your flag runner for any hits he or she might have before the runner hangs the flag. Under nearly all tourney rules, if the player who hangs the flag is found (after the hang) with a hit on him or her, the team will not get the credit (points) for the flag hang. In addition, the team might get penalized! This is not the place to get into all the tourney rules about playing with a hit on you, but you should be aware at least that you must study the rules of any event you enter.

- Don't keep paint pods half full if you can help it. They are noisy to carry, and the paint is likely to break from bouncing around. Topping off a teammate's hopper is an easy way to get that loader empty. Pouring paint into your loader only to find out that you had a broken ball or two in your pod can be a quick trip to a disappointment.

- When you have used a squeegee to clean paint out of a 'gun, hit a tree or barricade with the squeegee to knock off the excess paint. Ask a referee if you can wipe the squeegee on your camos in an inconspicuous location such as your armpit or the inside of a leg. Make sure the paint is rubbed in well, so a different referee will not be tempted to consider it a hit. Never wipe a squeegee on the ground or hit the ground with your squeegee. You will pick up dirt that can scratch the barrel or cause you more barrel breaks than you would have had with paint in the barrel.

Get a Routine

When you are on a team, develop a routine and go through the routine with your teammates. Your team should have one routine for the staging area and another one for the flag station before a game starts.

- In the staging area, before players head for the field, make sure all loaders and hoppers are fully loaded. It is actually common for a player to get on the field only to find that he forgot to fill up his loaders.

- Check your constant air tanks to make sure they are full and turned on with no leaks. Take an extra barrel plug onto the field with you in case you or a teammate loses one. Clean off all old hits before a new game.

- At the flag station, ask quickly whether every player knows his or her assignment(s) and objective(s). Make sure your head-protection system is on securely. Check that hopper agitators are turned on. When it's time, check that barrel plugs are out.

- Have timers ready to start when the game begins. When you are in a tourney, you may want a flag station routine that has one player actually call out a checklist. If you have time, part of the routine can be to review quickly any codes or signals—or at least remind everyone to use the codes.

Communication

Games are won by good communication. Learning how, when, and what information to communicate is one of paintball's challenges.

Once you are eliminated, no matter what you know, it is against the rules for you to pass that information to another player. Say you spot a crawler on your side of the field. It does no good for you to get picked off by that crawler before you verbally or silently give a signal to someone else on your team to say "I have a crawler at my 12 o'clock about 30 yards out." Therefore, you need to learn to talk it up on the field as much as you can. If one team member gives out needed information, make sure it reaches *every* team member. When the field is large and you're not sure you can be heard across a large distance, use hand and arm signals. Also use hand signals when stealth or remaining undetected in cover is needed.

A neat trick is to designate another color armband besides your own and your opposition's. This eliminates doubt when you try to identify a player. An opponent might give you false information and tell you he or she is your color. But if your color is blue and your opponent's color is red, you could

When you spot a hidden opponent, tell your teammates where he is before he shoots you ("dead men can't talk").

designate white, black, or some other color as your code color. Now any other color except the code color will come from your opponents. Change the code color after a couple of games.

Game End

When a game is over, the Game isn't. Challenges continue, and learning to master them will make your on-field game sharper.

- After a game, make sure your barrel plugs are inserted. Go directly to a check-in station if there is one. Get your team together, get ready for the next game, and then, if you have time left, critique the game you just finished.

- When you prepare for the next game, you should also follow a routine. Check each other for hits everywhere, and reload your hoppers and loaders. Make sure you have enough CO_2 or compressed air. Inspect your eye protection. You can rest and critique in any remaining time.

Practice these techniques on a regular basis and they will become second nature. You should soon see a difference in your game. You, too, can become a better, more formidable player.

Cleaning a Lens

Among the off-field challenges are those involved with keeping your gear in top shape. Seeing well is a big part of paintball, so here are a few words on your goggles and headgear.

- Suppose you play with goggles with a single lens. A thermal lens, for example, has an outer lens (the single lens) and an inner lens that will easily scratch. Cleaning paint off a single lens is easily done if you spray either plain water or the manufacturer-recommended lens cleaner onto the lens. Then use a soft cloth to clean the lens. This works well for light splatter. If you've been "gogged" and have a lot of paint goo on the lens, start by wiping off nearly all the heavy goo with a soft rag. Then spray the water or cleaner on the lens and proceed as with splatter. If you spray a lens that has a lot of paintball fill on it, the goo and the liquid will run into the grooves on the mask, making it harder to clean the mess out of the grooves.

- If you have really heavy paint on the lens and it has run into the grooves in the mask, you may find it is easier to remove the lens from the goggle, carefully clean it—first with water and then with lens cleaner—and put it back into the goggle. This is a skill best learned at home. It's a good idea to clean your lens after every time you play, which gives you practice removing and replacing the lens.

- When you need to clean a thermal lens, remember that the inner lens is a very soft plastic that scratches easily. Using a paper towel to clean that inner lens, for example, can scratch it. JT USA has a new microfiber cleaning cloth that is soft enough to clean the thermal lens without scratching it. You can use that, or well-washed and worn cloth baby diapers, to keep from scratching that inner lens. When you can't see as well, you don't play as well.

- Never put any substance on any goggle lens unless the manufacturer has approved it for such use! The lens is sensitive to damage from various chemicals, including those in Windex and other glass cleaners, alcohol, and various other cleaners. You won't see the damage that is done to the lens as the chemicals weaken it—but in the past certain lenses have been damaged to the point that a paintball shooting under the legal speed limit has gone straight through them. Use only what the manufacturer recommends.

- If your goggle lens is a single lens (not a thermal lens) and you are having trouble with its interior surface fogging up, your first choice should be the antifog material recommended by the goggle manufacturer. Consult the instruc-

tions that come with the goggle to find out what is recommended.

- If you don't have any antifog, you can try putting a few drops of a liquid dish detergent on the inside surface of the lens. Spread it evenly (you may need to add a few drops of water to get the detergent to spread well). Gently buff out the excess and streaks with a fine cotton cloth until the lens is dry. This should minimize or eliminate fogging. You can also try this on your prescription glasses.

- Another antifogging hint is to wear a sweatband so sweat from your forehead doesn't trickle down into the space behind your goggles. A folded bandanna will also work. Sometimes something as small as a piece of paper towel folded over your nose will reduce fogging. When you try these, be sure that the goggle foam remains in good, secure contact with your face so that it can work as designed for protection from a hit or splatter.

Cleaning Off Paint

Remember the words of wisdom about cleaning off your old hits? Paintball goo and shell (the shell is gelatin, like vitamin casings) can be cleaned off your skin, equipment, and clothing with water, soap and water, or rubbing alcohol. Do not let the alcohol get on a goggle lens! You may find it easier to take a spray bottle full of your choice of liquid, squirt a little on the paint, and then wipe the paint off.

When you're cleaning the inside of a barrel, water or soap and water are the best choices.

Avoid putting alcohol inside the barrel if it has a special coating that alcohol and other solvents may weaken or remove.

Get a dowel rod and a soft, bristled cleaning brush to assist your cleaning. Brush Research Manufacturing makes a nylon brush (called the NAM Power) that is effective for manual cleaning of barrels and other tube-type openings. I often use little 'gun-cleaning patches made of cotton. I do not recommend paper towels inside the barrel, as some paper is rough enough to scratch a treated inside surface that you find on some barrels.

Those are a few tricks of the trade. The more you play, the more you will learn little tricks that make the game more enjoyable. The more you learn, the more you will grow as a player.

33

Closing It Out

Jim "Roadrunner" Fox

Do you want to know how teams win games, which leads to a consistent string of wins, which wins tournaments? Teams win because they know how to *close out* (finish) their games. They execute maneuvers, eliminate players, and get the flag pulls and hangs—all within the allotted time.

Winning teams do not hesitate or run scared when a game is winding down. Many a game is won or lost in the last minute or two of a contest. A team that just sits there and does nothing in those closing minutes will lose. Teams that make things happen, those that push and always think offensively, have a better chance of winning most of the time. Moves that win games can also occur in the beginning and middle of a contest, not just at the end, but great closing teams don't panic if they are down a few players or their paint is run-

ning low. Teams win because they can overcome hardships, misgivings, or any other diversions that cause setbacks during a game.

Focus

You must stay focused at all times during your games. I have seen good teams start out great, play a good middle phase, but lose it at the end because they didn't know what to do or how to do it. A team is nervous mainly at the start and end of a game. In the middle phase, teams usually settle down, surveying the situation and making sure all team members are informed of it. Communication must also occur at the start and end of a game, but it is more consistently done during the "lulls" in the action.

Stay alert to opportunities.

As the end of the game approaches, many teams lose focus, start running out of paint, have paintguns go down, and have players eliminated. Winning teams anticipate and react to these inconveniences with confidence and poise. They plug up holes left by eliminated players; they take key bunkers or areas of the field. Teams look for, or try and make, an opening that will lead to the collapse of a flank. After that, the push continues and teams on the move can often back-door the rest of the opposition. It may, however, take three-fourths or more of the game to get to that point.

Victory

Make sure you know how much time is left in the game. Communicate with your team members. Know what a maximum score is and try to max out, to receive as many points as possible. Make

Winning is a team effort.

sure you have the flag in your possession, and check your flag runner for hits before he or she hangs the flag.

A lot of times the tide of victory is turned by a key move or single elimination made by one or more of your teammates. That move can come at any time during a game, so a winning team must stay focused throughout an entire game. Always think offense. Once the tide turns, actions such as moving, communicating, keeping your fire up, and eliminating or pushing back your opponents will make it easier for you to close out games. To be successful, to win games and tournaments, a team must always play to win, not just play not to lose.

Play to win.

Gearing Up

IV

Buying Paintball Gear

Action Pursuit Games staff

Many tournament players waste hundreds, if not thousands, of dollars buying gear they won't use and don't need. They'll purchase a new 'gun or some accessories with the expectation of improved performance only to discover that the "upgrade" doesn't enhance, and might even detract from, their playing ability.

This is a common mistake, but it's a mistake you don't have to repeat if you take a practical approach to buying tournament gear. Read on if you want advice on how to save money while selecting the best equipment to take your game to the highest possible level. Begin by answering these three questions about the type of tournaments you intend to play in:

How much paint will you use?

The number of rounds you anticipate shooting per game determines the size of your power source, the capacity of your loader and harness, and to a lesser degree the type of paintgun you need. NPPL players routinely shoot 1,000 to 2,000 rounds in a game, and a high rate of sustained firepower is a key tactical advantage of their style of open fields. Conversely, the paint limit is 200 rounds a player per game at PanAm circuit events, which makes mobility as important as firepower. While you'll need a big cylinder and huge harness to compete in the NPPL, the extra weight and bulk becomes a liability (and even a waste of money) when you play in the PanAm.

Will you play in cold- or warm-weather events?

Temperature also affects what kind of power source you need. If you play only in warm-weather tourneys, where the temperature stays above 60 degrees, you do not need to get a high-pressure (HP) gas system. You can save several hundred dollars by sticking with a CO_2 power source.

Will you play in one-day local tourneys or multiple-day national tourneys?

You won't need a lot of extra gear and spare equipment if you play only in local one-day events. A single set of clothing, a single spare lens, a single set of pads will get you through. Conversely, a big, multiday tournament requires double the amount of certain items and, most likely, a carrying case suitable for airline travel.

Answering these questions defines the parameters of the tournaments you'll attend, which brings your equipment requirements into perspective. Next you're ready to pick the type and quantity of gear you'll need. Use these three guiding principles to focus your choices:

1. *Small is good.* Lightweight and low bulk increases mobility and improves handling characteristics while decreasing target size. When choosing between two pieces of comparable-quality gear, opt for the smaller, lighter version.

2. *Make sure it's big enough.* The amount and capacity of gear must match the parameters of the competition. For instance, your power source must be equal to the number of paintballs you carry on the field. You don't want to run out of gas before you run out of balls.

3. *Don't under- or overspecialize.* Versatility is nice, but trying to be too versatile can reduce your competitiveness. As an example, some tournament players buy large-capacity harnesses, figuring they can just remove tubes for limited-paint play. In theory it sounds versatile, but on the field it's not competitively practical. An eight-pack harness is too bulky for

games where the paint limit is 500 rounds, especially when the competition is running around with compact three-pack carriers. An example of overspecialization is the player who bought a 44-cubic-inch cylinder for 200-round-limit, 5-man games and a 53-cubic-inch cylinder for 500-round-limit, 10-player games. The 10 percent difference in size cost the player about $200.

Here is the master list of equipment you need. We'll look at each item separately from a practical standpoint.

- Tournament-tuned paintgun
- Power source
- Loader
- Complete goggle system
- Harness
- Squeegees
- Tools and spares
- Travel case

Paintgun

A tournament-quality paintgun must be fast-handling, accurate, reliable, and consistent in its velocity. All these attributes are necessary, and you should compromise as little as possible on these features. The reason Automags and Autocockers are popular tournament-level paintguns is because they (each in its own way) both combine all these necessary attributes at a reasonable cost.

Do not buy a 'gun that is too heavy, feels awkward, or is difficult for you to shoot well! In tournament paintball you have to be able to shoot fast to score hits, but good handling characteristics generally take priority over rapid, sustained firepower. If you like the balance, sight picture, and pointing characteristics of a light-weight Spyder or Tippmann, then stick with it for tournament play.

Don't talk yourself into buying an ultracustomized, ultraexpensive Angel or Shocker just because other players say they are better paintguns. *Better for whom?* The only important factor that makes one paintgun better than another is whether you personally can play better with it. Comparing a standard Autococker with an STO illustrates this point. The more expensive STO comes with more tournament features, but many players don't like the STO's centerfeed. For them the standard 'Cocker with its unobstructed sight picture is the "better" paintgun.

Accuracy primarily is a question of matching barrels to paintballs. You do not need a half dozen different barrels; usually two will do. You'll be ready for year-round play with a small-bore barrel (about .684 inch) for cool, dry weather and a big-bore barrel (about .689 inch) for warm, damp conditions. Since almost all of the top barrel makers offer different bore diameters, finding a set is easy. Another enhancement for accuracy you should consider is a barrel reducer (available from, for example, LAPCO and J & J). The reducer screws onto the chamber end of a barrel and prevents small or out-of-round paintballs from rolling down the barrel.

A paintgun's reliability is more a question of the user's knowledge than the manufacturer's expertise. Most of the popular paintguns (they wouldn't be popular if they weren't reliable) are built well enough to survive tournament play . . . as long as you, the paintgun operator, understand how the 'gun works and how to maintain it.

Depending on the design, you may have to add quick-strip screws, pins, and bolts to make onfield cleaning quicker.

Power Source

Consistent velocity is an absolute must for a tournament-level paintgun. If your paintgun's velocity drops during a game, your range and accuracy will diminish. If your velocity jumps during play, you'll lose points at the chrono.

Warm-weather tournament players who use CO_2 need either a remote system or an antisiphon tube to prevent liquid from getting into their paintguns. Liquid CO_2 causes erratic expansion spikes, which cause velocity jumps. Along with a remote setup or antisiphon tube, every tournament paintgun should have an in-line regulator to control the pressure of the gas before it enters the paintgun's chamber. An expansion chamber is not the same as an in-line regulator. You need the reg.

When the temp drops below 60 degrees (F), an HP gas system changes from a luxury into a necessity for tournament competition. High-pressure atmosphere and nitrogen are not temperature sensitive like CO_2, which means HP gas won't freeze up your paintgun or decrease its consistent velocity in cold weather.

The downside of HP is cost, bulk, and weight. For the same number of shots, an HP cylinder is almost twice as big and about five times as expensive as a CO_2 bottle. Plus you have to purchase and maintain your own supply cylinders (scuba tanks) if your local field doesn't do HP fills. The good news is that the price of HP systems keeps dropping. Fixed output valve-cylinder combos are particularly appealing because they screw into the same adapters as CO_2 bottles. You don't have to buy special hoses, adapters, and mounting systems. This reduces the overall cost as well as the weight and bulk of the total system.

Loader

The closest things to a performance monopoly in paintball are the VL Revolution agitator loader and the EVlution agitated loader, both from Viewloader. At this writing, no other loaders are as fast or dependable. The only decision tournament players need to make is which model to choose. Equally important but often overlooked is the loader's connecting elbow. The adjustable types work best and are worth the few extra bucks they cost. Once you find the model you like, buy two or three extras.

Goggle System

Every tournament player should have two sets of goggle head-protection systems ready to go. If you take a shot in the lens, you can't afford to waste precious time between games disassembling and cleaning them, then waiting for the antifog treatment to cure before you can do the reassembly. Murphy's Law dictates you'll have back-to-back games and need to work on your paintgun right after you take one in the lens. Two goggles allow you to clean up at your leisure during long breaks between play. Here's a tip if you like playing with tinted lenses: set one up for bright sunlight (smoke color) and the other for twilight (yellow or amber).

Whether to go single lens or thermal is a toss-up. Thermal lenses resist fogging better, but they aren't as visually clear of distortion, and they're almost impossible to clean quickly without scratching. Nonthermal lenses are much more scratch-resistant, thus easier and quicker to clean. But they fog up, even when antifog treated. If you like the JT brand of goggles, the answer is to use a single lens in combination with a fan for maximum clarity, cleaning ease, and fogging resistance.

Harness

Paintball carriers keep getting better. The latest generation, built like a weightlifter's belt with open-end tube slots, is the most comfortable and versatile ever. The open-end slots allow you to change the size of your feeder tubes from 100-rounders up to 200-rounders, effectively doubling the capacity. For the ultimate in versatility, check out the new modular, zipper-attached packs. This innovation allows you to increase or decrease your paint load by zipping on or off pouches.

Squeegees

There are two ways to go with squeegees: the push-through stick or the pull-through cable type. The Straight Shot stick squeegee is particularly effective on Autocockers. Just pull out the bolt, stuff a piece of paper towel in the hole, and push it all the way through the chamber and barrel for a one-step cleaning. The problem with the stick is where to keep it. Strapped to your calf or attached to your bottom-line cylinder, you have to be careful not to catch it on a bunker.

The cable-type squeegee, which you can coil up and stuff in a pocket, is much more convenient to carry. And the model with the cotton swab on the end is great for cleaning out the feed port or a ball break in the chamber. But cable-type squeegees have one glaring problem: They can't push a tight-fitting ball out of a barrel. So you have to make sure you fire your 'gun to clear it before you remove your barrel for cleaning. You need several squeegees with swabs to get you through a day's play: once the swab is covered with paint, which it will be after one good cleaning, you have to wash and dry it before you can use it again.

Tools and Spares

Here is where the smart tournament player can really save money. More bucks are blown on unnecessary repairs, tune-ups, and modifications than in any other area. For less than the cost of a typical anodizing job, you can buy a complete set of tools and a comprehensive selection of spare parts to keep your paintgun operating at peak performance for at least two seasons of tournament play.

Paintguns are relatively simple machines. There's no reason why a tournament player with the average intelligence of a fifth grader can't learn to fix his or her paintgun. What stops most players is a resistance to learning. They're willing to buy the tools and parts (if they know what to buy), but they're not willing to put in the time and energy to study their paintgun's operating system.

Here's how to go about it. First, read the manual (several times). Second, buy the video (almost every 'gun manufacturer offers one). Third, call up the company and ask where to go for an airsmithing lesson. Most manufacturers offer seminars or can refer you to a competent airsmith in your area who can teach you.

Outfit yourself completely, including spares, for a tournament.

Travel Case

Tournament play means road trips, and whether they're by car, train, or plane, you're going to need a good, practical case to transport all your gear. Here's what to consider before you buy:

1. Make sure the case is big enough for all your playing gear, including your shoes. Nothing is more frustrating than to drive out to a field and start setting up to play, only to realize you've left one critical piece of equipment back at the hotel packed away in another bag.
2. It needs a good lock. This will keep baggage handlers out of your stuff and stop your teammates from "borrowing"

your gear when you're not around and they can't find theirs. Also, it's a known fact that tournament players perform better on the field when they know all their expensive equipment is secure back in the staging area.

3. The case must be strong. At the tournament it will be used as a chair, table, and workbench. It will get knocked over, thrown around, and covered with oil, paint, dust, and mud. Soft-sided luggage just doesn't cut it. The gear inside isn't protected enough. You need a hard case.

4. It needs wheels. A case big enough to carry all your gear is too heavy and too bulky for you to carry comfortably.

Backup

Once you have all the essentials, it's time to consider a backup paintgun. For players who know how to fix their 'gun, a backup is a luxury. For those who don't, a backup is an expensive necessity.

You'll need fewer tools, spare parts, and accessories (barrels, elbows, etc.) if the backup is the same type of paintgun. You'll also be familiar with its operation and handling characteristics, which will lessen the impact to your playing performance if your primary 'gun goes down.

A good solution from a practical, cost-efficient perspective is having a team backup paintgun. The cost of a tournament-tuned paintgun is divided among several players. This is most effective when the majority of players on a team shoot the same type of paintgun.

Final Advice

Don't go to a tournament expecting to buy essential gear that you need. Often vendors show up late or leave early, which means they won't be there when you desperately need something, right now, before the next game begins. Also, vendors quickly sell out of crucial items. They'll have plenty of hats and T-shirts when you need a replacement for your cracked grip frame. ("Sorry, we just sold the last one about five minutes ago.")

Clothing, Pads, and Shoes

Currently, less than half of all tournament players wear camouflage. BDUs have been supplanted with uniforms of jersey-style top and pants, usually in a dark shade for some concealment in shadows. It's ironic that teams began moving away from camos because they wanted an easy-to-recognize, distinctive-looking uniform for their teammates. Now all the teams are starting to look the same again.

Whatever design of uniform your team picks, choose colors or patterns that are easy for you to differentiate. You should be far more concerned with the problem of friendly fire than with the benefits of blending into the bush you're hiding behind. Stalking, ambushing, and other tactics that require a high degree of concealment do not have a significant role in tournament paintball.

Knee pads and shin guards should be considered mandatory protective equipment for paintballers. Everyone should wear them; the only question is whether you wear them under or over clothing if the tournament gives you that choice. JT's neoprene pads work best under clothing. They conform to the knee joint, and won't slip when you're running, crawling, and sliding. The exterior type from JT, Trace, GOG, Renegade, Red's Comfort Gear, and other brands offer more protection for shins. The exterior style is more popular, but that's because most tournament players are more concerned with protecting their uniform pants than protecting their knees.

Most tournament players wear football-style shoes with soft cleats. This design of shoe offers flexibility for running, some ankle support, and good traction in loose dirt and grass. The downside of football cleats is they seem to wear out about one week after they break in. An alternative is the new generation of hiking boots that manufacturers have introduced over the last couple of years. The latest models are as light and flexible as football shoes, offer good traction and ankle support, but are much more durable.

Expert Advice on Buying a Paintball Gun

Michael "Grizzly" Grubb

"I am an active paintball player and am looking for a new 'gun. Maybe a semi-automatic. I am in the price range of $150 to $250. I want a 'gun that is easy to maintain and put back together. I also want a good, reliable 'gun that works in extreme cold weather (20 degrees and up). I can't decide."

"I have just started playing paintball and have rented a 'gun every time I have gone out. I have looked through your magazine several times for a 'gun. What kind of 'gun would you recommend?"

"I played about three games and am now going to buy a paintgun. I have about $300+ to spend. I am looking for a semiauto with lots of upgrades. I hope you can tell me the truth. It would also help if you were to make some sug-gestions. My needs are accuracy, ease of operation, many spare parts or upgrades, and very long range. I have always wondered why some 'guns are so expensive ($600) and some are so cheap ($90)."

"I am 15 years old. I am a constant reader of your magazine and I find the articles very interesting. I have been playing the sport of paintball for only about four months, but I love it. I do not own my own 'gun but I would very much like to. I was wondering if you could give me a few suggestions about how to find a good quality, semiautomatic paintball gun."

As these letters say, buying a 'gun runs high on the list of "Things to Do Right Now." Longtime player and airsmith "Grizzly" Grubb offers his advice here. If you expect him to tell you to buy the Sluggo because it's the best 'gun, forget it. He won't tell you what to buy. He does share a few secrets, though.

Grizzly's Secrets

Throughout the 15 or so years I've been involved with paintball, I've seen some of the most sensible people make some of the must unsensible choices when they purchase their first paintball-throwing hot rod. More often than I care to remember, I have seen someone come into a store ready to spend whatever money it will take to buy the current "hot" paintgun, when he hadn't yet even played his first game! Excited to the max from just "watching a game," already he's reaching for his wallet. How many people would buy a race car just because they watched a car race? Too many in paintball do the equivalent of that. Before you make a poorly thought-out purchase, before your choice leads to frustration instead of enjoyment, consider these recommendations.

Test-Drive the 'Gun

My first suggestion: Before you even consider buying a paintball gun, play at least two or three times. Play with whatever paintgun you can rent or borrow. Many times I've asked people who haven't even played yet but are hyped on the game why they are so sure they want to spend money on something they've not checked out for themselves. I ask, "Can you really be sure that this game is something that you will want to stay with for some time to come?" Most will say "Yes!" no matter what.

Sadly, though, some of these people will use their newly acquired equipment maybe once or twice, and then will put it away because things didn't turn out like they expected. Their paintball gun either ends up being sold for cheap and the ex-owner is not happy about paintball or, even worse, a beautiful 'gun gathers dust and rust in a remote part of the garage or closet. Make sure your interest is really there before going out and spending money on any gear, in any sport.

Heads Up

My second suggestion: Get headgear before 'gun. You can't play in this or any other sport without items that keep you safe and healthy. A goggle and facemask head-protection system designed and manufactured for paintball is an absolute must to protect you well. You want to buy a 'gun, and that's great, but you'll become a better player when you can see well out of your own new, unscratched lenses.

Be sure to buy something that will cover your ears and protect them sufficiently from the direct impact of a paintball. This will avoid possible damage to the ear. Think about other sensitive areas, including the throat, sides of the neck, top and back of the head, and the groin. There are numerous commercial products made to protect these areas.

Check It Out!

My third suggestion: When you go out to play, look at the setups used by other players. Ask them about their paintball guns. The playing field can be one of your best sources of what is hot and what is not.

On most any field you can find two dozen different makes and models from an array of manufacturers and customizers. If you see something that attracts your attention, you might just go to the player between games or during a break and ask the individual to tell you what he likes or dislikes about his setup. If you offer to replace the paint, many players will let you shoot a bit to see how that particular setup feels.

Now, bear in mind that most players will tell you that what they are shooting is really the "best of all." They are attached to their favorite pieces, just as to a pet. Take what they say with a grain of salt. As you check out different 'guns, you may very well change your mind several times before spending your money. That's better than buying a 'gun you later find out you don't like.

What's Your Game?

My fourth suggestion: Think about your game. Is it stock or semiauto? If you were to spend your money on a decked-out 68-Automag, you would be straight out of luck if your friends all play stock 49 weeks of the year.

What's your position or role on a field? If you're a Robbie Newbie, you, like most newbies, may not be able to start at the top of the heap. No matter what you try, when you play against more experienced players, you can expect to suffer quite a few quick eliminations. Don't blame the 'gun if you're almost the first player out all day. Try to find a game with less experienced players. Then you can get used to the 'gun without being overwhelmed with new things in the game.

In a game, of course, not everyone does the same thing. Some players go for the flag. Others guard their own flag. Some hide in heavy brush, where a shorter barrel might snag less than a longer one. Others tend toward open areas, where a longer barrel might add accuracy for a longer distance shot. Buying your 'gun is some-

thing you want to coordinate as much as you can with your game.

How you play will be the biggest factor in determining how happy you are with the 'gun you purchase. Over time you might change your style, but you probably can adapt the 'gun for your new style of play.

Fumblefingers?

My fifth suggestion: Consider whether you are a person who is mechanically inclined. If you are not willing to break out the toolbox to work on a home repair, you will most likely be the same way with any paintball gun you own. If you are Mr. or Ms. Fumblefingers, you should best look for a 'gun that needs as little maintenance as possible. Or else find a qualified airsmith to work on your 'gun . . . and be ready to pay well in money or time for the airsmith's services.

On the other hand, if you are the tinkering type, you will probably be able to buy a 'gun that might be considered "a bit more temperamental" among paintball circles. When you ask around, you'll hear which 'guns are for the tinkerer and which are rough-and-tumble and almost never need attention beyond a cleaning.

Flag Hang Time

A purchase of any type can be made well or made poorly. The amount of homework or research you put into the purchase will almost always determine how happy you will be with it. Even though it might be tempting to run out and buy the most expensive 'gun you can find, remember: The 'gun won't do the job for you. The 'gun works only as well as you do. It will take some time, no matter what you end up buying, before you have the experience necessary to get the most out of any paintball 'gun.

Don't be like Robbie Newbie, the new player who took his newly bought paintball gun back to the store, complaining about it because he was shot out early in every game. If Robbie Newbie had known, as you do now, that his best weapons in the game are practice and experience (not how much he spent on a 'gun), he would have been happier.

36

How to Choose a Used Marker

James R. "Mad Dog" Morgan, Sr.

All you folks who have played a few games and find you really like paintball well enough to start saving up the money for your own equipment, one way to save a few bucks is to buy a used paintball marker. As you've looked over the shelves of your local pro shop or drooled through the advertisements, you've probably seen that good markers usually go for quite a sum of money when they are new. To save a little money so you can actually play the game, too, you've probably thought of picking up a used paintball marker. However, you have undoubtedly worried that if you aren't careful, you could be saddled with a lemon. Take heart.

The benefits of getting a used marker are many. First is the price. Many previously owned paintball markers sell for 50 to 60 percent of their cost new. Second is the fact that most used markers come with great optional accessories— for well under the cost of getting them yourself. (Some of these aftermarket accessories, such as special valves and bolts to increase performance, can't be seen without taking the marker apart; others, including aftermarket sights, barrels, and grips, visibly stand out.) Third, since the marker has been used, you won't cry as much when it gets a scratch or ding on it as you play.

Plenty of good, reliable used paintball markers are out there. In fact, a lot more of the tournament tricked-out Autocockers and Automags are showing up in the used market since the advent of the Angel, Bushmaster 2000, and other electronic markers. Another reason that good used markers are available is that many players suffer from burnout (as in all sports) and leave the sport, giving you a chance to pick up a good, functioning marker at a bargain price.

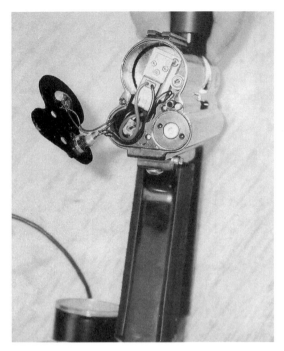

Upgraded internals raise the value of a used marker.

As with all things that you buy, there is a Buyer Beware Factor.

Types

For newer players, first a word about what type of paintball marker you should be looking for. Once, long ago, a beginning player could take a pump marker into a walk-on game and have a reasonable chance of doing well. But (unfortunately, in my opinion) those days are largely past. With the proliferation of many budget-priced semiautomatics and today's lower paint prices, the semiautomatic should be the first choice of today's newer player.

Open Bolt

For beginning players, I always recommend a good, durable, open-bolt semiautomatic. There

are different models of them, including Spyders, PMI Piranhas, Tippmanns, and many others. This type of paintgun marker has been around for years. Parts and add-on extras are plentiful. They are much simpler than other types to clean and maintain. And, importantly, they take a good amount of punishment and neglect and can still fling accurate paint at an opponent. Very often, what you rent at the field will be an open-bolt semiauto. Fields do sell their rentals from time to time, too, a possible source you may want to explore.

Used markers can be good buys.

High End

Are you thinking about getting one of the top tournament markers, such as the Automags, Minimags, Autocockers, Sovereigns, Typhoons, or what I call "graduate" markers (Angels, Shockers, and other electropneumatic markers)? Be aware that some of these high-end markers require more care and maintenance than the simpler semiautos to get peak performance.

A good idea, in addition to getting the owner's manual, is to buy an aftermarket guide

Check the grip fit as you shop for a used marker.

(book or video) for the marker you purchase. (These are available for many markers.) The combination of information, working with your local airsmith who should have experience on these models, and factory assistance, if needed, will help you learn your marker and correct any problems.

In your search for a used marker, you may be offered a deal on one of the new high-end electronic markers, such as a Shocker or an Angel. These are capable of throwing a lot of paint down the field very fast. Most players who get these markers won't part with them, so if you aren't buying from a reputable source, my advice is to check the manufacturer's list of stolen markers.

Airsmith

I highly recommend locating a good paintball airsmith in your area. The seller should not mind if you have the airsmith check the marker before you buy it, just as when you take a used car to a mechanic for a check before you make your decision about whether to make that purchase. Although many aftermarket add-on accessories for paintball markers are simple do-it-yourself items, the adding on of other accessories, such as mounting an anti-double-feed, is really work for a qualified airsmith.

Installing something incorrectly could wreck a marker and be unsafe. If the marker being sold has been modified by machining, you might not be able to make other modifications to it ever again. Consulting a good airsmith is always a good idea. When you have met an airsmith who's well qualified, you have a person to go to anytime in the future if you encounter a problem that you can't fix. Most paintball pro shops either have certified airsmiths on staff or can refer you to an airsmith in your area.

Playing Time

The advice I usually give brand-new players is to stick with the less expensive semiautos until having played for at least a year. This lets them get some playing time under the belt, learning how to play effectively.

As you will find out, paintball is as much a thinking game as a firepower game. To state the point simply, "You don't have to outgun what you can outwit."

How to Buy

Here is a summary of tips for purchasing a used marker.

1. Choose a model that you commonly see at the fields where you play. The more commonly used it is in your area, the easier it will be to find repair parts, previously owned upgrades, and a qualified airsmith who is familiar with that model.

Never buy a paintball marker made by a manufacturer that has gone out of business. Repair parts or accessories will be nearly impossible to find. A qualified airsmith should be able to give you this kind of information. However, it is usually all right to buy a model of marker that is discontinued if it was made by a company that is still in business. Tippmann, Worr Games, and Palmer's Pursuit, for example, will still get you parts for markers they aren't currently making.

2. Ask about the marker's history. When did the seller buy it? Was it bought new? Ask for the original packing box and owner's manual. It's

worth asking for the original purchase receipt also (though not getting it is not enough reason not to buy). Ask what aftermarket modifications and parts are on the marker. You might also want to know where the marker has been used, such as in special big games or tournaments.

3. Ask why it is for sale. If it's been in the closet for "a while" you would want to check with an airsmith before you buy it. If you see the person using it every week at the field and know he or she just bought a new marker, that should raise your comfort level.

4. Buy a .68 caliber paintball marker (unless you are a collector, or have a ready source of paint in a different odd size). The other sizes of paint can be hard to come by.

5. Check the production date and any subsequent hydro-testing dates. Check the dates for the air cylinder, CO_2 or compressed air. CO_2 tanks over three inches in diameter must be hydrostatically tested every five years, and a composite (fiber-wrapped) tank must be tested every three years. If the tank is "out of hydro" ("out of date"), it should not be filled until it is "hydro'd."

Most paintball stores will accept your tank and have it hydro'd. The store sends the tank to a testing facility at a cost to you that might be as high as $25, and the process can take from a couple of days to three weeks or even longer.

Also check the tank for scratches, cuts, or dents. If the tank is taped or has stickers on it, these should be removed to check for damage to the tank. Here again, having an airsmith take a look can be helpful.

Test-drive a used marker before you buy.

6. Shoot the marker in a target area. Shoot paint through it before you buy it. A marker may "dry-fire" well, but hate having paint in it. If you're really serious about buying a marker, run at least 200 paintballs through it before putting down the money or plastic.

7. In your testing, include chronographing. First, dial it into your field's speed limit, which outdoors should be 280 to 300 feet per second (fps). The marker should be able to hold steady in that range over a dozen or so shots, with fluctuations of 10 fps or so being acceptable. If it can't be adjusted to do that, it needs to visit an airsmith, preferably before you buy it. A marker that is erratic in velocity is not only inac-curate, but also could disqualify you from playing. If it goes over the field limit on the pregame chrono, the field won't let you into that game.

Second, shoot a string of a dozen balls, one right after the other. Chrono one ball before you start, and chrono the last ball you shoot. Look for the difference. If it's over 15 fps different, find out why before you buy (you may need to consult an airsmith).

8. Feel around for loose or wobbly parts. Carefully check the feed ports (especially power feeds), grip frame, and hose connections. Broken feed ports are expensive to repair, and stripped screws are common on some models. Look through the removed barrel into a light.

Learn about a marker from the manufacturer.

Test carefully before you buy a used tournament marker.

Look for scratches, dents, or other irregularities. Older barrels can be smoothed and polished using a *Flex-hone*, which an airsmith can do. As an alternative, you can buy a *Flex-hone* player's kit and do this yourself. If the barrel has two parts, check for looseness between them. Look at the barrel when it is on the marker: it should hold a straight line from the body of the marker to the muzzle of the barrel, not bending slightly where they connect. Look from all around the marker to check for barrel fit and alignment.

9. Have the owner show you how to field-strip the marker. This will do two things. First, it will show you the proper method to clean the marker. Second, it will give you a chance to examine the internals of the marker more closely.

Then reassemble the marker and shoot it again, just to be sure you put it back together right. About those internals, besides the obvious ones (look for parts that are rusted, corroded, chipped, scratched, etc.), ask the owner if these are after-market or factory-standard parts.

10. And, lastly, if you're not completely satisfied with the marker, don't buy it. Don't let a salesman give you that ol' "It was only used on Sundays by a little old lady from Santa Fe Springs who just used it on the target range" routine. If the marker isn't up to standards or isn't what you want, then find another one that is. Or, save money to buy the marker you want new. Whatever you decide, play clean, play hard, and keep your goggles on or the plug in!

How to Stay on the Leading Edge of High-Tech Gear

Jim "Roadrunner" Fox

What does "high tech" mean in paintball? High tech can range anywhere from a new, state-of-the-art product to something you did to modify your equipment yourself. When we think about something being high tech in paintball, usually we think of the paintguns and paintgun accessories, such as air lines, expansion chambers, regulators, barrels, and hookups. Usually high tech is something designed to give the player more of some characteristic or ability—flow rate, distance, speed of loading, accuracy, consistent velocity. These kinds of high-tech items are advances for every paintball player. They are on the cutting edge of paintball's evolution. I'm talking about state-of-the-art gear and custom or signature series gear.

But to me, and to nearly every player I've ever talked to, high tech also can be anything that makes the game easier or more enjoyable for

you. In other words, it can mean anything that is "better" than what you have now. Here, I'm talking about both mods a player can do for himself to move up the high-tech ladder and methods of play that every player and team can learn.

High tech is anything better than what you had.

Even if you are on the absolute leading edge of technology, you have room to move up the high-tech ladder. There's always one more step to take.

State of the Art

A brand-new product for sale to the paintball player is a state-of-the-art high-tech product. For example, the new paintguns that use electronics are high tech. The WDP Angel, made in the United Kingdom, with its regulators, electro-pneumatics, and custom Viewloader VL2000 agitator loader, is definitely high tech.

How does a player locate these state-of-the-art products? A good starting point is looking at the advertisements that distributors and manufacturers place in *Action Pursuit Games* magazine. Contact the advertisers, get their catalogs, visit their websites, go see the new gear at your local store or field.

In addition to the new electropneumatic paintguns, high tech includes the new regulators that are smaller, multistage, and higher pressure than older models. Regulators control the pressure of the propellant going to the 'gun. With a consistent pressure, the player can expect to get a more consistent velocity and more predictable performance from a 'gun. Some regulators handle all of the current propellants (CO_2, N_2, and compressed air), whereas others may work with only one type of propellant.

The newest in motorized hoppers offer new motor and gear drives, different ways of turning the agitator on, more and different battery configurations, and so on. These are high tech, too. State-of-the-art changes to existing products can be high tech. New venturi designs for bolts (to

High-tech head-protection systems

smooth the airflow) and the use of new materials (polymers and metals) fall into this category. Remote systems with new-style, quick disconnects; downstream bleed offs; the 4,500-psi, high-pressure air bottles; and new mounting systems are all part of the high-tech frontline. High tech also applies to the newest in goggle and head-protection systems, paintballs, barrel design, electronic sights, valves for tanks and pressure gear, and the new constant-air CO_2-fill valves and system from Tippmann.

Signature Series

Custom paintguns and "signature series" paintguns are another category of high tech. This category is associated almost exclusively with paintguns. While simple cosmetic changes to a 'gun (such as painting or polishing) can be done by many owners, the more serious changes, such as splash anodizing or immersion coatings, must be done by professionals. Splash involves one kind of process and can put multicolors on a paintgun; immersions are often done in a trademarked pattern, which may be a camo pattern.

Performance, custom work on internal paintgun parts is another high-tech area. This kind of work should be done only by a qualified airsmith. What makes this work worth buying is the expertise of the airsmith, who has spent many, many hours learning just what custom work will improve the 'gun's performance. You're paying for his capability (know-how) and resources (tools, machinery, parts).

A signature-series item is designed by a well-known person in the paintball sport. The person may have invented the particular item or may have come up with a special modification that makes this item work better than standard products of its kind. Or the item may be something that the celebrity uses in tournament play, and the person is known for being on a world-championship team.

High-Tech Mods

A player can do many things to modify or enhance equipment and make it more high tech relative to what he or she had before. Here's where "high tech" takes on another meaning. What is high tech to one player may be yesterday's news to another.

An easy high-tech move is to replace standard factory screws and allen screws with stainless steel ones to prevent rusting. If you make the substitution, be sure to get the exact replacements. Adding a little clear nail polish or Locktight 242

(the nonpermanent kind) stabilizes screws so they don't work loose when you don't want them to. Using small O-rings with some screws, as when adding an O-ring at the barrel threads, helps keep things screwed in tightly. Covering the opening on your power feed with a clear piece of tubing or rubber, secured with a zip tie, can often effectively block one of the ways rain and dirt can get into a paintgun. The covering must be loose enough to let "blowback" vent out the opening.

An emergency fix is a piece of duct tape, perhaps three inches long, with one inch folded back on itself, sticky side to sticky side. This leaves one inch of sticky surface for attachment and one inch to act as a nonsticking flap over the opening. A coat of car wax carefully applied to the exterior of your paintgun may make it easier to clean.

A new barrel with a different inside diameter or other change in design might give you better performance. Aftermarket bolts with different performance characteristics are available for many 'guns.

It's high tech to have more than one air tank. For CO_2 tanks, this allows one tank to be warming up after a fill while you use the other one. It's also high tech to switch from a 7-, 10-, or 12-ounce CO_2 tank to a 20-ounce tank, and this makes it less likely that the tank will ice up and cause a serious drop in gas pressure (and velocity).

Have you tried a sight? That's an instant way to look high tech, especially if you go with one of the red-dot, adjustable-brightness sights (e.g., from ADCO). But even a $15 sight will make you more high tech than players who don't yet use a sight. Having the right repair parts and knowing what to do with them are definite necessities for the player who wants to be known as high tech. Some of the aftermarket kits have O-rings made of more durable materials than the stock O-rings, another step up the high-tech ladder.

A sight gives a high-tech look.

High-Tech Play

Even the way you go about playing paintball can be high tech. You'll look and be high tech if you use team codes, dress as though you are pros, and play in a professional manner. Practice as if you were in the finals of a tournament. Videotape your practices and games, and review the videos as a team. Critique each game as soon as you get back to the staging area.

Work on being a complete player. Learn to be a good low crawler and a player who knows how to hold a wire for a long time, one who is respected for making the hard push when that has to be done. Know how to be the floater who needs to have a picture of the whole game. Be able to shoot and play bunkers both left-handed and right-handed.

High-tech players usually practice and play in the same type of camo pattern. If you use one pattern in practice and another in play, the visual difference in your teammates may slow your reaction time down in a game just where it is critical. Other teams use different camo patterns when terrain or weather conditions dictate, counting on the advantage of better camouflage to offset the additional recognition time that may be involved.

High-tech players use a timer of some kind. Timers range from ones with multifunctions to a digital stopwatch or a talking countdown timer from Radio Shack. The timer needs to be where you can see and hear it easily. Many players mount their timer on the hopper or hopper lid.

High-tech players know how to run their 'guns at the cutting edge of speed. When you need to dump paint on a position, you need to do so with snappy effectiveness. This means knowing the fastest way to operate the trigger. For many players, using the middle finger instead of the index finger is fastest.

Making a great move can make you look high tech.

Uniforms look high tech.

Your playing ability and equipment won't become high tech overnight, but you can work at moving up the high-tech ladder. It will take time, effort, knowhow, and expense. In the end, you will become the most formidable paintball player that you can be.

Tomorrow's High Tech

The best way to stay in touch with the latest and move up the high-tech ladder is to stay involved with the game: (1) Visit your local store regularly. (2) Read *Action Pursuit Games* magazine. (3) Keep your eyes open at the field. (4) Talk to the local airsmiths. (5) Get to know the local tournament players—they see more of the cutting edge than nearly all recreational players; talk to them about gear. (6) If you can, get to the major events and trade shows. Even if you don't play, you will see a lot of high-tech gear there, either at the vendors' booths or in use on the field.

The latest harness and biggest pods are high tech.

Twenty-Six Tips for Buying That New Paintgun

Action Pursuit Games **staff**

"What is the best paintball gun for me to buy?" Every player who gets into paintball is going to ask that question sometime, at least once. There are dozens of paintball guns on the market, and every player has his or her opinion on which one is the best. Here are bits of advice that will help you make your decision, collected by APG's staff by interviewing players, store owners, and paintgun manufacturers.

1. Talk to others. Find 10 people who own the kind of paintball gun you think you want to buy. Ask them what they think about the paintguns they own.

2. Be a smart consumer. Not all paintguns are alike. There are big differences in the quality. Spend time finding out about quality, so you get the best quality for the money you have to spend.

Ask other players how they like their markers.

3. Get good advice. Ask people who have played for a while what they think are good choices for the climate where you play. Also ask the field airsmith what he or she thinks about different paintball guns.

See what experienced players shoot.

4. Read information you get from the store or the manufacturer.

5. Test-shoot the paintgun before you buy it.

6. Decide what kind of game you like to play in. If you like the stockgun games, get a stockgun. If you want to play constant air, go CA.

7. Buy a paintgun for where you like to play. You want to be able to use your 'gun at the fields you like. If they don't allow full-auto, or if they are pumpgun only, that would influence your choice.

8. Decide on your price range. Do this before you get serious, and then see what choices you have in that range. Don't forget to look at used 'guns.

Test-shoot a paintgun before you buy it.

Check out used markers, too.

13. Talk to someone who has owned more than one paintgun. Find out what they replaced and why.

14. Play with several different paintguns before you buy.

15. Look at the high-end paintguns. See what features they have. You may want to

9. Do your homework before you buy. Get a 'gun that will do the job you need it to do. Some people buy the least expensive 'gun then aren't satisfied, and right away feel they have to buy a better one. There's nothing wrong with an inexpensive 'gun if you only play a couple times a year, but for heavier use, you may need a more expensive one.

10. See what you can upgrade on a 'gun. You can start with a small budget and add on later.

11. Learn about the 'gun before you buy. You can get information about paintguns from sales people at the stores, other players, ads in the magazines, and the field staff.

12. Talk to people you see working on their own paintguns at the field.

Play a few games with what you're thinking about buying.

You and your paintgun should be one.

make that investment up front, especially if you are moving into tournament play as fast as you can.

16. Test the paintgun at the range. If you see someone with a paintgun you're thinking about buying, ask him or her if you can shoot it a few times at the range. Ask questions about its maintenance.

17. Consider the weather you play in. If you play in cold weather, get a 'gun that runs on compressed air or nitrogen, and buy that kind of power system. Be sure your field has refills available. You will pay more, but you will have a 'gun you can use year-round. Otherwise you won't be able to play when the weather gets cold because CO_2 doesn't work well in the cold.

18. Get on the Internet. You will find out way more than you ever wanted to know about any paintball gun that's on the market.

19. Find out about maintenance. Remember that you are going to have to take care of your paintgun. Find out how to clean it, what replacement parts you need to have in your toolbox (O-rings, for example), and how to adjust the velocity.

20. Check the fit. Ask yourself before you buy whether the paintgun feels comfortable when you pick it up. Is it too big for you? Do you need a stock? Will you need a remote system for it?

21. Check it again. Consider the grip, length, weight, sights, trigger pull, trigger fit, balance, and stock length to make sure you are comfortable with each.

22. If you want to play stockgun games, be sure the 'gun can be used in those games. Your 'gun will have to run on at least 12-grams. Some 'guns can be converted to stock and back to direct-feed pump, and from 12-gram to constant air.

23. Look at the owner's manual. Does it have good, easy-to-follow instructions? Is there a diagram of the parts?

24. Inspect the barrel. Remove the barrel and look through it while you hold it up to a light. See if it looks smooth and polished.

25. Find out what the price includes. Remember that you will need a power source (bottle and hoses) and a loader, so see if the price includes these.

26. Ask yourself, "Do I really like this paintgun?" This may be the most important question you ask. You are going to spend a lot of time enjoying it, so be happy with what you buy.

No matter what paintgun you shoot, play safely. Wear approved goggles, chronograph regularly, play only at safe speeds, follow the rules of safe paintgun handling, and keep the game fun.

39

High-Tech Barrel Theory

Russell Maynard

The first high-performance barrels date back to the "rock 'n' cock" era of the mid-1980s. Back then, a few enterprising do-it-yourselfers discovered honing and polishing the tight bore of a stock paintpistol would dramatically increase both range and accuracy. Crude but effective, a good honing-polishing job on those short factory barrels with a brake-cylinder hone, sandpaper, and steel wool produced an additional 50 fps of velocity and considerably smaller group sizes at 30 or 40 yards. Back then, before chronos were common, the players who knew about this technique had a decided advantage.

Well, barrel technology sure has come a long way. The perpetual paintball quest for more range and better accuracy has spawned a huge market of specialty barrel makers. Just thumb through *Action Pursuit Games* magazine and call a few stores. You will find barrels available in almost any length, type, and style, with just about every imaginable combination of features, finishes, and materials. With so many to choose from, the problem for today's players is figuring out which barrel is the right one to buy.

It's a problem because most players don't know anything about barrel technology. And making the problem worse, most players take as gospel what they hear from other players or what they see in advertising. Well, this may come as a shock to you, but some of the claims made in some ads are a little inaccurate . . . about as inaccurate as the barrels those companies sell. And as for the technical advice from that "expert" parked next to you at the field, too often his wisdom, insight, and vast experience on the subject is no more informative than "You should buy this barrel because I did."

Which brings us to the focus of this article: What follows is a short guide to barrel technology. There are no recommendations or opinions on this or that barrel in this article. I am not going to tell you which barrels I think are good or bad (so don't turn to the last page looking for a quick answer). What you will find is a lot of theory, information, and testing procedures. You will have to think your way through all this, but once you understand how barrel design, materials, and manufacturing techniques affect range and accuracy, you will be able to decide for yourself which barrels are high performers and which are just hype.

Spin Factor

Understanding *why* one barrel performs better than another begins with examining *how* a barrel affects the range and accuracy of a paintball in flight. The first rule to learn is "Spin is the enemy of accuracy." If a paintball starts spinning as it shoots down the bore, it will curve when it exits the muzzle and enters the atmosphere. The faster the paintball is spinning, the harder and quicker it will curve.

Ever wonder why paintballs hook and twist out of a wet barrel? Here's what happens: One side of the ball skids across the paint puddle in the barrel (just like a bald tire on wet pavement), while the other side drags along the surface of the bore. Within a fraction of a second the paintball starts spinning fast enough to tear itself apart inside the barrel or, if the ball manages to stay in one piece, to come curving out of the muzzle like a spastic Frisbee.

Spin happens because a paintball is round and because it has a seam. Changing the shape of paintballs would help solve the spin problem and give better accuracy, but other factors prevent bullet-shaped paintballs from being practical. It's

been tried and didn't work. Because a paintball is round, the slightest amount of uneven surface friction between the shell and the wall of the bore will start the ball rotating. And once out of the barrel and flying through the air, a spinning paintball (like any ball with a seam) will curve off its line of flight because of the aerodynamic forces being exerted across the surface of the ball.

Like a baseball or tennis ball, a spinning paintball will rise, sink, curve, or corkscrew depending on the speed and direction of the spin. In fact, because paintballs are not perfectly round spheres, because they have a single, relatively prominent seam, and because they have a liquid fill inside a flexible shell, the effects of spin are much more dramatic with a paintball than with a solid, round ball.

Testing Spin

If you want to test what spin does to accuracy, shoot some of those paintballs with two-color shells. You can see the spin of the ball, and you'll notice two things: First, "no spin" (which causes the paintball to act like a knuckleball) is as bad for accuracy as "too much spin"; and, second, a small amount of forward or backward rotation is common (and beneficial because it helps stabilize the direction of the ball's flight path toward the target).

The spin factor is why some open-bolt semis have less than stellar accuracy. When the bolt slams forward and pushes the paintball into the breech (the part of the barrel closest to the ball drop), the ball still may be rotating when the released gas hits it. A slight rotation caused by the bolt's impact can turn into spin as the gas launches the ball down the barrel. This is why a soft bolt push, a tight breech, and a ball-detent system that helps control the direction of the spin all make a big positive difference in accuracy with open-bolt semis.

The spin factor also is the reason that some shots seem to hit harder. When a fast-spinning ball impacts and the shell ruptures, the liquid fill (which also has spinning momentum) spreads outward in a swirling arch, which dissipates the force of the impact. But when a slow-spinning paintball impacts, the shell and the liquid fill act like a two-stage, cone-shaped charge to focus the force into the target. (This is when you get those nice ring-shaped hickies we all know and love so much.)

Bore

Now that you understand the spin factor you can see why the second rule is "The bore is the key to accuracy." The bore (bore hole) is the inside of the barrel from end to end; the paintball touches the bore. A well-made bore controls the rotation of the ball and directs its flight path without retarding the paintball's acceleration.

If (1) the bore hole is straight, symmetrical, and matches the size of the balls you are shooting (more on this match later), and (2) the bore is clean and the surface finish is consistently smooth to prevent uneven drag, then the paintball will glide down the bore with very little spin and fly out of the barrel with amazing accuracy. On the other hand, when all or any of these conditions are present, accuracy diminishes: if the bore hole is not symmetrical, if the size of the bore does not match up with the size of the paintballs you are shooting, if the bore is dirty, or if the surface finish is uneven. Then the ball will skid, twist, and spin down the bore and fly out of the barrel with equally amazing inaccuracy.

This is why so much effort goes into controlling the dimensions of the bore in a high-performance barrel. A slight deviation or imperfection within the bore can cause uneven friction, which will start the ball spinning.

Shaping the Bore

A paintball barrel begins as a tube of raw metal. The tube usually was formed in one of three ways: (1) Most aluminum tubes are extruded, (2) stainless steel and brass tubes may be drilled out of bar stock, and (3) sheets of stainless and brass can be rolled and welded into cylinders. If you cut any of these raw tubes in half lengthwise and magnified the cross section 100 times, you would see waves of high and low areas along the wall of the bore. Those little hills and valleys vary by as much as plus/minus .005 inch.

Five-thousandths of an inch may not seem like much deviation, but it is enough to make the difference between a very inaccurate, low-end barrel and a very accurate, high-performance product. The reason is that those high and low spots in the wall surface can cause uneven friction as the ball slides down the bore, which will create spin.

Polishing an uneven bore surface does not eliminate the high and low areas; it just makes them smooth and shiny. For maximum accuracy the bore must be machined to make it a straight, perfectly round bore hole.

Bar Honing

The methods manufacturers use to make the bore walls symmetrical also set the size of the inside diameter. The most common method is called *bar* or *shaft honing*. A bar hone is a steel rod with honing stones set in three groves running along its length. The shaft turns like a lathe as the barrel is pushed over it, and the honing stones (which can be adjusted to the exact diameter desired) grind off metal to form a straight, round hole. Bar honing can sometimes leave an unevenness that can be made even by use of the patented *Flex-hone* tool. The *Flex-hone* should be used before the final finish (hard-anodizing, nickel-plating, etc.) is applied.

The trouble with bar honing is that it must remove metal to make the bore walls symmetrical. If the inside diameter of the raw tube is big to begin with, bar honing isn't a practical method of achieving symmetry.

Swaging

The other way to straighten the bore is to *swage* the barrel. Swaging doesn't cut metal. Rather, it compresses metal. One swaging method locks the barrel into a machine while a steel ball is pulled or "drawn" down the bore. The ball squeezes through the hole, shaping the bore to its exact diameter. In another swaging method, called *roller burnishing*, a steel mandrel is placed inside the tube while powerful rollers compress the outside of the tube. The softer barrel metal is crushed onto the mandrel by the rollers to shape and size the bore.

Most paintball barrels that have "rifling" or ridges in the bore are shaped by swaging. The mandrel has cuts in its surface, into which the barrel metal is crushed to form the ridges. If the mandrel is twisted slowly as it is drawn, or if the mandrel has spiraling grooves along its length, the bore of the finished barrel will have spiral rifling.

ID/OD

A player should know about the inside diameter (ID) of a barrel and the outside diameter (OD) of a paintball, because matching the ID/OD will affect accuracy and performance.

Barrel ID

Even if the bore is perfectly symmetrical, a barrel won't shoot well if the paintballs don't match the size of the bore. The barrels on the first factory paintpistols were designed with an ID of .685 inch to match the OD of the .68 caliber paintballs. But, as mentioned earlier, airsmiths and aftermarket manufacturers found that enlarging the barrel ID to around .692 inch reduced excessive friction and increased range and accuracy.

These opened-bore barrels worked fine in spring and summer, when paintballs swell a little, but in fall and winter cold, when paintballs shrink a little, the big bores were worthless. (I well remember a cold October tournament in Nashville several years ago when West Coast teams with their big-bore barrels couldn't shoot straight. When they pointed their 'guns down while slowly cocking the pump, all the balls lined up in their feeders would roll through the chamber, down the bore and out of the end of their barrels!)

The better barrel makers learned the importance of matching ID and OD, and today high-performance barrels are available in three general sizes: Small (tight) bores are .684 to .687, medium bores are .688 to .690, and large (big) bores are .691 to .694. From a performance standpoint you may not notice a big difference between a small and a medium, or between a medium and a large, but you definitely will notice the difference between a small and large bore, especially when the weather is either very cold or very hot. A few thousandths of an inch can make a huge difference.

Paintball OD

If all paintballs were perfectly round, and if they all came in one size and stayed exactly that same size, we wouldn't need barrels with different ID sizes. But paintballs are not all made to the same specifications, and it wouldn't make any difference if they were—because paintballs constantly shift shape.

Paintballs are as changeable as the weather. They swell and turn rubbery in heat and humidity, then shrink and become brittle in cold, dry air. The only thing constant about the dimensions of paintballs is that they constantly are in a state of change. Result? The paint you bought last week that shot so well in your new barrel is now double feeding, occasionally breaking in the bore, and curving off high to the right. Because paintballs change, knowledgeable players own barrels with different IDs.

Testing ID/OD

It is important to have a match between the ID of a barrel and the paint you intend to shoot through that barrel. You can quick-test a paint and barrel OD/ID match by putting a paintball into the breech and blowing it through the barrel like a blowgun. If you cannot blow it out, the barrel is too tight for that paint (or you need to quit smoking). If it rolls out the barrel when you tip the barrel earthward or if it blows out the barrel easily without any compression, the bore is too big for

that paint. But if there is just enough friction to get a good seal and pop the ball down the tube, that OD/ID match is just right.

For another informative test, spray foot powder down your barrel and shoot a paintball through it at about 250 fps. If the ball's OD matches well with your barrel's ID, the ball will maintain two thin, consistent lines of contact along the wall as it glides down the bore. These lines of contact will be 180 degrees apart. This shows you there is equal friction on both sides of the shell, which means the ball is not spinning down the bore.

Small Bore If the barrel ID is too small for the paint, the contact areas will be much thicker. If the ID/OD match is way too tight, you will see signs of the ball touching in more than two spots or sealing tightly like a cork in the barrel.

As a general rule, a little tight is better than a little loose. If the ID is slightly small, you will lose a little range and gas efficiency but keep most of the accuracy. If the ID is very small for the paint, expect to lose range and accuracy, to have fluctuations in velocity, and to have problems with balls breaking at the breech.

Big Bore Going back to the powder test, if the barrel ID is too big for the paint, the lines of contact won't run symmetrically down the bore. There will be interruptions in the lines (like skid marks) or a series of zigzag smudges caused by the ball skipping from one side of the bore to the other as it bounces and spins down the barrel.

If the ID is a little big for the paint you are shooting, expect to double-feed balls and to see the consistency of your velocity turn erratic. Your accuracy will be less consistent too, with occasional balls noticeably curving off target.

If your barrel's ID is way too big, your paintgun will double-feed most of the time, your accuracy will seem like you have paint splooge in the barrel even when it's dry, and you occasionally will have balls breaking halfway down the bore as they rupture from bouncing against the wall of the bore. A ball detent may help with the double feeding, but it won't improve your accuracy. A tighter ID barrel is a better solution.

Breech Steps

One technique barrel makers have employed to compensate for the shrinking and swelling of paintball OD sizes is to create a step in the breech. A step allows a barrel to shoot a wider range of paintballs accurately. The step is a smaller ID area left in the first inch of the breech when the rest of the bore is enlarged. The step area is tight enough to prevent medium OD paintballs from double feeding, yet short enough not to create excessive drag with larger OD balls. For example, with a step in the breech at .689 inch and the rest of the bore honed out to .692 inch, one barrel can cover the ID ranges of both a medium- and a large-bore barrel.

Barrel Reducers

The latest concept in steps is the "barrel reducer." It is a short section of barrel, about an inch long, with a tight .685-inch ID. The reducer has male/female threads to screw between the breech end of the barrel and the paintgun's chamber area. A barrel reducer gives the same effect as having a step in the barrel. You use the barrel reducer when shooting paintballs with an OD too small for your regular barrel, and then take it off to shoot larger OD paint. But since reducers usually have a very tight ID, you can shoot smaller OD paintballs with it than you can from most step-down barrels. It is a pretty simple, effective, and cheap way to extend your barrel battery.

Smooth or Even Finish

The surface finish of the bore is critical to accuracy. An even finish in the bore is more important for accuracy than is a smooth surface. Don't confuse the two.

An even finish throughout the bore is necessary to maintain a consistent amount of friction on both sides of the shell, which prevents the paintball from spinning. The surface must be consistently even and clean, with no deep scratches, ridges, burrs, or patches of smoother and rougher metal. A smooth finish comes from a combination of the type of metal used (some metals can be polished smoother than others; for example, brass can be polished smoother than aluminum) and the degree of polishing to the surface.

Smoothness is beneficial because it produces less friction. A barrel with a smooth finish can have a slightly tighter ID without a noticeable decrease in range and accuracy. This means a smooth small- or medium-bore barrel can shoot a broader range of paintball sizes. For example, a .689-inch, nickel-plated barrel can shoot a range of paintball sizes that would require both a medium-bore barrel and a large-bore barrel if made from aluminum. That is because a nickel-plated surface is smoother than an aluminum surface.

Here's an example of the difference between smooth and even. A hard-chrome surface is at least ten times smoother than a hard-anodized aluminum surface, and a brass surface is at least five times smoother than a hard-anodized surface. But if the finishes on all three surfaces are equally *even*, the range and accuracy levels of the barrels all will be fairly equal too.

Periodically, barrels can be lightly polished with a NAM Power or a Final Touch polishing tool. As a barrel wears with use, it may develop scratches, tiny pits, smooth and rough spots, and so forth.

Barrel Materials

The two metals most commonly used for making barrels are brass and aluminum. Both are relatively inexpensive, easy to shape, and fairly corrosion-resistant (important when dealing with the condensation inherent to CO_2). Aluminum has the advantage of being lightweight. The advantage of brass is its smoothness.

On the downside, both brass and aluminum are "soft" metals that scratch easily and quickly lose their even finish. Aluminum can be anodized for durability, which is a process that hardens the top surface of the metal, but the anodization must be a type-3, "hard" anodizing if it is going to be hard enough to resist scratching. The type-3 process leaves a relatively rough surface that is too hard to polish as highly smooth as raw aluminum (this is the reason that some manufacturers anodize the outside but not the inside of their barrels).

Harder metals can give the high-performance benefits of both a smooth *and* an even surface finish. Stainless steel is an excellent, but expensive, choice—providing you don't mind the weight. Another option is coating or plating the surface of brass or aluminum with a hard chrome, electro-

less nickel, or other specialized material. Hard plating with a chrome-nickel alloy works well, providing it is a hard "industrial" finish and not a soft "cosmetic" finish. A hard-plated surface is as scratch resistant as stainless steel, polishes to a higher level of smoothness than brass, and can be coated onto a lightweight material like aluminum. The downside to plating is the difficulty of doing the process correctly. If poorly applied, the plating can have uneven thick- and thin-coated areas or can chip and flake off.

Range

Now that you understand how the barrel affects accuracy, it's time to look at what affects range. Let's begin with Rule #3: "Velocity is the major factor in how far a ball will travel." If you secure a paintgun in a padded vise so the barrel is exactly six feet above and perfectly parallel to a flat plane of ground at sea level on a windless day, an average-weight, standard-shaped paintball exiting the barrel precisely at 300 feet per second (fps) will travel approximately 50 yards before it hits the ground. If you increase its velocity, the paintball will travel farther; decrease its fps and the ball won't fly as far. Once a paintball stops accelerating, the pull of gravity and the friction of atmosphere slow it down and pull it to the ground at a fixed, predictable rate.

Does this mean the only way to increase range is to raise velocity? And once you reach 300 fps, what then? Are you stuck with everyone else or is there a way to get an advantage? (No, cheating the chrono is not the answer!) There *is* hope. All else being equal, including velocity, some barrels will shoot a little farther than others. How is this possible? The high-tech answer to that question requires first understanding how your paintgun's valve affects a paintball's acceleration down the bore.

Spike Pressure

Note: Carbon dioxide (CO_2), the most common paintball propellant, is used in the following example, but nitrogen and compressed air create much the same effect. When you shoot your paintgun, the exhaust valve opens and a small burst of CO_2 is released. The compressed CO_2 begins expanding, traveling about the speed of sound, toward the paintball waiting for it in the breech end of the barrel.

Depending on the temperature (the higher the temperature, the greater the pressure), the CO_2's pressure as it exits the valve chamber ranges somewhere between 450 and 1,400 pounds per square inch (psi). But by the time the expanding CO_2 reaches the ball, its pressure has dropped to between 50 and 100 psi. This is the amount of pressure that shoots the paintball, and it is called the *spike pressure*.

If the spike pressure is below 50 psi, there won't be enough initial force to propel a paintball up to the normal velocity range of 250 to 300 fps. But if there is much more than 100 psi of spike pressure hitting the ball, it almost always causes the shell to rupture, thus "blowing up" the paintball in the barrel.

The spike pressure is critical because a paintgun's barrel functions as both a guidance system for the ball *and* as an expansion chamber in which the gas expands to accelerate the ball. Consequently, the specifications (especially the length) of the barrel you choose must match up with the spike pres-

sure of your paintgun for maximum performance.

Paintguns with valve systems that produce spike pressures in the upper range, 75 to 100 psi, accelerate a paintball quickly with a short burst or "pop" of gas. Paintguns with lower spikes (50 to 75-psi range) "push" the paintball down the barrel; they release a longer duration of gas, and the ball accelerates slower.

In the pumpgun category, 'guns with Nelspot-style valves are "poppers"; Sheridan-valved-style 'guns are "pushers." And in the semi-auto class, several markers have low spike pressures, whereas nearly all blow-back-style 'guns (Spyders, Tippmanns, etc.) have higher spike pressures.

Barrel Length

For maximum range you must match barrel length to the type of paintgun you use, but you don't have to be exact. To guide a ball in a straight line you need a minimum of about 5 inches of barrel. The rest of the barrel's length should be just long enough for the gas pressure (either a "pop" or a "push") to accelerate the ball the entire length of the bore and out the muzzle, but the barrel should not be so long that the paintball begins slowing down before it leaves the muzzle.

All other factors being the same, paintguns with higher-pressure spikes should use shorter barrels (6 inches to 10 inches) while those with lower-pressure spikes should use longer barrels (9 inches to 13 inches). Here's why: After a paintball exits the bore and the propulsion effect of the CO_2 ceases, the ball stops accelerating. There is nothing you can do to make a ball in flight go faster. What is controllable, though, and therefore critical, is the acceleration of the ball while it still is inside the bore. If the ball still is accelerating as it leaves the barrel, you get slightly more range. If the ball is slowing down *before* it leaves the barrel, you get slightly less range. This can be verified by putting two chronographs in line (one after another), about 10 feet apart, and shooting over them with different barrels at the same velocity. A ball shot from a barrel that accelerated all the way out of the muzzle will lose less velocity by the time it passes over the second chronograph than a ball that started slowing down before it left the barrel.

Too-Short Barrels If the barrel is too short for your paintgun, the ball won't be directionally stabilized enough for good accuracy beyond 20 or 25 yards. A too-short barrel also will require a higher CO_2 spike pressure to develop quick acceleration of the ball, which can cause ball-breakage problems.

Also, if your paintgun's valving cannot produce a higher spike pressure, a short barrel can prevent you from getting the velocity up to an acceptable level (especially in hot weather). And if you adjust your valving to release more gas, you'll be swapping one set of problems for another. With too short a barrel, your CO_2 efficiency will go way down and your paintgun will bark loud enough to attract wild coyotes and refs with chronos. Plus, the excessive amount of gas blowing out the barrel around the sides of the paintball has an adverse effect on accuracy (see "Porting," which follows).

Too-Long Barrels If a barrel is too long for your paintgun's valving type you will have less range, less CO_2 efficiency, and erratic velocities. The ball will be slowing down before it leaves the muzzle, and more CO_2 will have to be released to overcome the added friction. More gas plus a longer rate of expansion equals more variation in velocity from shot to shot.

One more note about barrel length is in order. If you just can't be happy unless your barrel is extra long or very short, you can compensate to a degree by selecting a bigger or smaller bore ID. A slightly larger bore on a really long barrel reduces the excessive drag, while a slightly smaller bore on a shorty barrel helps control the expansion for improved acceleration of the ball.

Porting

The newest innovation in barrel technology is porting. Smart Parts gets the credit for taking the concept to the mass market, and in one form or another just about every high-tech barrel now incorporates porting.

Porting does two things: First and foremost, it quiets shots by spreading the sound of the escaping gas over a longer duration. Second, porting can improve accuracy by reducing the effect of gas turbulence on the ball.

At the moment when the ball exits the muzzle, gas still pushing behind the ball can put uneven pressure across the surface of the shell, which as you know can create spin. (This problem is amplified if the tip of the muzzle, called the crown, is not cut at a true right angle.) Small port holes help prevent this by dissipating the excessive gas pressure. As a side benefit, the venting of excessive gas through the ports also helps maintain consistent velocities. But porting also can work against you in this respect by preventing the gas pressure from staying high enough in the bore to accelerate the ball up to an acceptable velocity range.

As a general rule, a tight series of small port holes at the end of the barrel are more effective for accuracy, while a spread-out series of small holes is more effective for quieting.

Range and Accuracy

Many players believe that a higher velocity means better long-range accuracy. They're wrong. While more fps equals greater range, pushing the velocity close to the 300-fps limit reduces the accuracy level of many barrels.

Each player needs to find the range-accuracy sweet spot of his or her 'gun-barrel-paint combination. Usually the sweet spot is somewhere in the range of 270 to 290 fps. Don't try to add an extra 10 fps for more range if it means losing consistent accuracy. It will work against you.

Practical, effective range is limited to how far you can shoot, hit the target, and get the ball to break consistently. You may be able to hit players at 50 yards, but chances are the balls won't break. In a game, when it counts, being able to hit an opponent's exposed loader or foot at 35 yards is a much better shot than bouncing a ball off his chest at 50 yards.

Comparing Performance

A good paintgun with a high-performance barrel and matching paint is capable of consistently hitting a soda can at 15 yards, a 12-inch plate at 30 yards and a two-feet-by-three-feet, torso-sized target at 45 yards. "Consistently" means 7 out of 10 shots. Because of its superior accuracy, especially at ranges beyond 30 yards, a high-performance barrel will seem to have much greater range than a low-end barrel. Additionally, compared with a cheap tube, a high-performance barrel will be able to shoot a much wider selection of paintball sizes with good (if not great) accuracy.

But the biggest advantage a quality barrel gives is its consistency. Because you know its trajectory and trust that it will shoot accurately, you will take the time to aim and make your first shot count. On the other hand, if your barrel is inaccurate, you won't be confident of hitting the target. You will be on the defensive, stuck in the spray-and-pray mode.

Head for the Store

Now that you understand the various features offered on high-performance barrels, upgrading your paintgun's range and accuracy is just a question of what your wallet can afford. Depending on the weather where you live, you probably will want to buy two or three different ID-size barrels and maybe a reducer.

Top-of-the-line chromed stainless steel or electroless-nickel-plated barrels, with honed or swaged bores, with porting and the rest of the works, retail for $75 to $150 each. Barrels with the same features but made from brass or aluminum are available in the $50 to $100 range.

Playing Stock and Pump in a Semiauto World

John Blair

Paintballers who use stock or pump markers in games against semis are used to getting "the Look." The Look comes from both newbies and experienced semiauto players alike. It says, "Are you NUTS?"

After all, you're walking into a game with folks shooting semiautos capable of throwing 5, 6, 7, and more paintballs per second your way. Even if you shoot a constant-air pump, even with an autotrigger, at best you can shoot only about half that (and none of those shots will be well aimed). If you're playing with a stockgun, the incredulity goes up a notch because you have only 10 to 20 shots before you have to reload (change tubes). Plus, there's that pesky 12-gram cartridge you have to change, and it's good for only 20 to 30 shots (fewer in cold weather) before it, too, has to be changed.

Nevertheless, there's nothing crazy about playing stock or pump in an open-marker game. It can make your game much more intense, challenging, and enjoyable. And, believe it or not, you

Stockgun players can hold their own against most semiauto shooters like this one.

can be very effective playing against the semis if you adjust your game to your marker.

Markers

A pump marker is paintball's chameleon. It can be a stockgun powered by a single 12-gram, with a horizontal feed (you have to rock 'n' cock it to put a ball in the chamber), holding no more than 20 paintballs. A pump also can be a constant-air marker with a 20-ounce tank, a 200-round VL2000 Shredder, and an autotrigger. Nearly all pump markers convert from 12-gram to constant air. A few of them can even be converted from pump to semiautomatic.

Pump players looking for the maximum challenge can keep their markers strictly stock. Pump players who want to "even the odds a little more" against semiautos can choose the higher capacity tank and loader to get a little closer to the semiautos.

Sneak or Storm?

When you play stock or pump against semis, you have to adjust your style to fit your relative lack of firepower. A "sneaking" game is often just the ticket. Sneaking involves moving slowly and carefully, watching and listening for movement that might clue you in to an opponent's position. What's in your favor? Semiauto shooters don't pay much attention to anything except the incoming paint from other semiauto shooters. Listening is something the semiauto players don't do well, partly because their firepower tends to make them play more aggressively and partly because they always seem to be shooting.

Moving more slowly does not mean that you will miss all the action. Some of the most exciting games this author has played were with a trusty 12-year-old Nelspot 007 stockgun, playing the sneaking game against semis. My favorite strategy playing with this limited-capacity old-timer is to wait in the background until the more aggressive players have made contact and established positions. Then I mosey quietly toward the action, staying low and listening to identify opponents' positions. Then I move in, carefully, and try to take a few players out. More than once I've opened up a flank this way, leading to a flag capture.

Sneaking

Especially on a crowded field (a target-rich environment, or TRE, in military-speak), just sitting quietly in one place can be very effective. Position yourself well, near a tape line or in a natural bottleneck where your opponents will be forced by brush or terrain to move through a relatively narrow area. Taste the incredible thrill of taking out an opponent with one shot—when he didn't even know where it came from!

If you're discovered or you run into more than you can handle, it's generally a good idea to retreat and try another spot. Going toe to toe with semis is not a productive strategy.

One-Shot Sneaking

A sneaker who takes the time to look and listen as he advances can often get very close to an opponent before taking a shot. At that point, fire rate or loader capacity is a moot point—one shot ought to be all you'll need. You can do this. A

Belly-crawling is easier with a stockgun.

player who is moving slowly or not at all is relatively hard to see anyway.

Pick one target and move in. On occasion, I have spent up to half of a game moving in for a good shot on one or two entrenched opponents, easing from bush to bush, crawling through low spots, until close enough for a guaranteed tag.

By choosing these tactics, you won't get to shoot much, but your shots will count a lot more often (and who can really complain about spending less money on paint?).

Group Sneak

Sneaking is usually a one-person approach to playing because it's hard to sneak around in a group.

You can set up multiplayer ambushes when the entire ambush party shoots stock.

Team Play

Stock and pump players can play effectively as part of a team. One of the most exciting ways designates the stock or pump player as a runner backed up by three or four semi-shooting teammates.

The squad advances in tandem. The pump shooter waits for the right moment to make a dash, either for the flag or toward a player or group that has been distracted by the semi-toting teammates. The pump shooter is not carrying all the heavy semiautos, heavy constant-air tanks, or heavy extra paint pods in a harness. The pump shooter carries only a light stockgun, a few tubes of paint, and some extra CO_2, 12-gram cartridges. The stock shooter can shoot with just one hand—leaving a hand free for grabbing the flag. It's surprisingly difficult to hit a running target, and it's much easier to run full-out, with nothing but a stockgun in your hand.

Speedball

A warning is important here: Playing speedball against semis with a stockgun is not usually a good idea. Most of the time there's "nowhere to run to, nowhere to hide."

Camouflage

Camouflage clothing is standard wear for players on most fields except for indoors and speedball. Stock and pump players who take on semis par-

Camouflage: a stockgun player's friend

ticularly need to wear clothing and gear that will help them stay hidden. Since stealth is so much a part of this sort of play, chromed markers and neon-bright T-shirts are probably not good ideas.

Paintballers who like to sneak get very serious about their camouflage, using camo greasepaint on all exposed skin and tying strips of camouflage cloth to their masks and BDUs. If you add strips of camouflage cloth to your outfit, or if you buy a commercially available ghillie suit for the same effect, check with your field and tournament operators to be certain that ghillied clothing is allowed (paint marks get hidden in the ghillie).

Practice, Practice

The average semiauto player does not do much target practice. Even team players, who practice tactics and play scrimmage games, only rarely go plinking. If you're going to play pump or stock against semis, you must target-practice. You need a natural sense of the sight picture so you hit your target consistently. Unlike shooting a semiauto, every shot counts when you play stock or pump. There's no "spray and pray" with a stockgun.

The Payoff

So when you enter a game with semiauto shooters and they all give you the Look because you walked up with that stockgun or that pump, just be patient. Your skill, your marker, and your tactics will give them *your* version of the Look. Off the field, after the game, several of them may appear a little shocked because they're wearing your paint—and just beginning to realize where it came from.

Your skill, a Phantom stockgun, and tactics: the Look